Grow Your Sales, Do What You Love

Mindful selling for entrepreneurs and freelancers

by
Anis Qizilbash

Copyright © 2015 by Anis Qizilbash. The right of the author to be identified as the author of this work has been asserted in accordance with the Copyright, Designs and Patents Act 1988. All rights reserved. No part of this publication may be reproduced or distributed in any form or by any means, or stored in a database or retrieval system or transmitted by any means, electronic, mechanical, photocopying, recording or digital or otherwise except as permitted by the UK Copyright, Designs and Patents Acts 1988, without the prior written permission of the author.

Limited liability/ Disclaimer of Warranty: While the author has used her best efforts in preparing this book, she makes no representations or warranties with the respect to the accuracy or completeness of the contents of this book and specifically disclaim and implied warranties or merchantability or fitness for a particular purpose.

Cover design: by Ritesh Ghosh

Front cover photo credit: amasterphotographer/ Shutterstock

ISBN-13: 978-1522821816

ISBN-10: 1522821813

DEDICATION

For my beloved Jennifer,
who always saw something in me
that I'm slowly beginning to realise.

CONTENTS

Copyright	ii
Dedication	iii
Introduction	7
Five obstacles faced by people new to sales	11
What you will learn	14
STEP 1: Ethos	17
Why this matters	18
Being present: How to avoid being the stereotypical salesperson	22
Your purpose: Unlock your most powerful source of motivation	26
Practise: Let your subconscious do the heavy-lifting	29
How to shift from negative to positive	31
Cultivate a successful seller mindset	35
How to stop letting competition make you feel insecure	40
STEP 2: Preparation	45
Productivity: How to spend more time where it matters	46

Physiology: Simple tips to perform at your peak ... 53

Planning: Where you're going and how you'll get there ... 57

Create a winning sales plan in seven steps ... 60

The entrepreneur's money magnet ... 67

Proficiency: How to punch above your weight ... 78

STEP 3: Investigation ... 83

Two intrinsic sales tools to help you investigate ... 84

The most influential conversation ... 86

How to ask questions ... 88

How to avoid sounding canned ... 93

STEP 4: Confirm ... 96

Don't drop the ball ... 97

When to make it about you ... 100

STEP 5: Add Value ... 103

How to talk about you and your product ... 104

Random acts of value ... 111

STEP 6: Contribution 113

How to avoid desperation 115

STEP 7: Take Action 118

Closing techniques: Helping your prospect say "yes" 121

How to avoid sounding "salesy" 126

What to do when a prospect says "no" 127

How to nurture prospects for the future 131

Onwards and Upwards 133

Innate talent is a myth 136

EPIC ACT: Your seven steps to success 138

Acknowledgements 141

About the author 142

Resources 143

Bibliography 145

INTRODUCTION

Nothing is impossible, the word itself says 'I'm possible'!

- Audrey Hepburn

Does the thought of selling make your toes curl?

Do you find yourself with business leads but can't seem to convert them into revenue?

Does self-doubt and nerves affect your ability to successfully sell and get paid for doing what you love?

If you find yourself whispering "yes" to any of the above, I wrote this book for you. Here, you'll learn a seven-step sales process to grow your sales and keep doing what you love.

I used to hate selling. I've met many entrepreneurs and freelancers who despise or fear selling so much that they procrastinate the selling part of the job. Or they rely heavily on repeat business and referrals, which means they have never before engaged in outbound proactive selling. But being overly reliant on referrals and repeat business will never give you the life you love or the freedom you deserve.

My intention with this book is to inspire entrepreneurs and freelancers to successfully sell so they can 1) carry on doing what they love without having to go back to a nine-to-five job, making money for someone else and 2) enjoy the freedom that comes with working for oneself. Why wait until you're 65 to spend quality time with your loved ones or travel the world when you can do it now?

From introvert to rate-card queen

I had a very sheltered childhood; I had little contact with people growing up, I wasn't allowed sleepovers or to have many friends and school discos were out of the question. Yes, we called them discos back then. So by the time I hit the work force, I wouldn't say boo to a goose! Shy and introverted, I had zero social skills and it pained me to talk to people.

Once I realised I didn't want to be a doctor - fainting during organ dissection during GCSEs kind of rules out medicine - I had to think of another vocation. A voice told me:

Learn to sell

Part of me thought it was insane. I can't sell. I can't even talk to people. But I listened to that voice and looked for sales roles.

I managed to land in the final round of interviews for a business-to-business sales role for Future Publishing, founded by TED curator Chris Anderson. I was shocked to make it past the first round, a group interview where I put forward the odd suggestion but generally remained quiet compared to bubbly, more talkative candidates. I didn't stand a chance compared to these people who were obviously born to be salespeople.

"Do you want to know why we picked you?" asked my future line manager when he called to invite me to the second round. "You were the only one listening and not talking."

On the first day of the job, they showed me to my desk. It had a telephone and 2 three-inch thick folders filled with files of contacts. That was it. My job was to sell advertising space at the back of a magazine to sole traders and small business owners. Every Thursday morning I scoured a weekly competitor magazine for fresh leads to sell them space in our magazine. If I didn't call before 11am, my competitors would have already called them. It was a gruelling nine months of call after call, rejection upon rejection.

When I moved jobs to a competitor, I was brought in as an account executive. I had three colleagues, also account executives. They were the stereotypical salespeople - overly confident and abrasive. They bullied me a little, making my new job horrible so I hated those early days. But I shut them up with my actions. I brought in new business at rate-card prices (i.e. "sticker" price with zero discount) and cross-sold products to existing clients.

Eighteen years later, I've sold to a wide variety of people in different sectors, from London's Tottenham Court Road traders to multinational companies, NGOs and government officials. I've sold across twenty countries, generating millions in revenue.

I'm not some superstar salesperson by any stretch of the

imagination. Far from it, in fact. There are salespeople out there who have raked in way more sales than I have and gone on to high-flying roles in Google. I had my dry seasons, where for a short spell I didn't bring in any sales. I also know why, experience I share in this book so you can overcome it.

Like you, I don't like "selling". I don't fit any of the typical salesperson stereotypes. People often tell me I'm too nice to be a salesperson, that I'm not a typical showboat.

I quit corporate sales roles because my passion lies in helping others succeed, people like you. I firmly believe a lot of societal problems would be solved if we all did what we loved. So I'm purposefully driven to help you succeed. There's one thing I'm good at and that's inspiring people; I see it in my coaching and workshops. It feels like my purpose. That's why I'm writing this book - to help more entrepreneurs and freelancers like you get paid well for doing what you love.

You've probably heard this before, but one of the biggest reasons businesses fail is a lack of revenue. I want to do my little bit by sharing with you the tips, strategies and practical wisdom you need to help you grow your sales so you can carry on doing what you love while being your authentic self.

Five obstacles faced by people new to sales

Stand up to your obstacles and do something about them. You will find that they haven't half the strength you think they have.

- Norman Vincent Peale

1. "I don't want to be that annoying salesperson"

What comes to mind when you think of a salesperson? Take a moment and scribble it down on a piece of paper. When I ask people this question, they usually use terms like "manipulative", "big talkers", "pushy" and "out for themselves". I honestly believe these feelings hold people back from wanting to sell; nobody wants to become that annoying salesperson.

This is the stereotype of an average salesperson, the one who actually gets in the way of successful selling. Why? Because they're chiefly concerned about themselves. They focus on competition, closing and commission. As buyers, you and I can sniff this out a mile away.

Can you remember a time when you were dissuaded from buying by a sales assistant at a retail store? They ask, "how can I help you?" but you feel something different. They want to usher you to the till or make sure you know their name so they get their commission - and they'll say anything to make that sale.

2. "I'm not extroverted"

Many people operate under the notion that a specific personality type is necessary to be a successful salesperson. Perhaps you aren't thick-skinned or optimistic or extroverted so you have concluded that you will never be good at selling.

3. "I don't know how to sell"

Unless you're in a sales role, there's a very good chance you don't know how to sell. Neither schools nor employers teach this fundamental life skill. Even people studying business and management aren't provided these techniques!

4. "Selling is beneath me"

Many people feel selling is beneath them. For the longest time I was ashamed of being a salesperson. It wasn't until I hit my late thirties that I realised how these skills helped me in life. And in the process of helping myself, I was helping other people get what they wanted.

5. They're just not that into you

Buyers don't care about you or your product, they only care about themselves. Sorry to break it to you, but they're just not that into you.

Helping you sell more

So the sales game is rigged. Buyers hate sellers and you hate selling. But if you can't get customers to buy from you, what will happen?

Not generating enough sales is the number one reason new businesses fail. It sounds obvious but clearly it's easily forgotten, given the way people speak of and run their businesses. Failure to generate sales means having to dust off your CV and getting back on the corporate treadmill, a cog in someone else's machine. If you're reading this, I know you don't want to do that.

I believe anyone can learn to sell. Contrary to popular belief, it is not a natural gift limited to those with a specific personality type. Yes, you need to learn to handle rejection - for which I provide you guidance later on - but you don't need to be a brash, chatty individual. I am certainly not a smooth talker. I suffer from foot-in-mouth disease - and I have big feet! But those times I tripped up worked to my advantage because it showed people I was normal and capable of making mistakes. Making others feel comfortable in who they are is critical to building rapport and rapport is the grease of the sales process.

I'm going to show you how to short-circuit the system so you can get buyers to buy from you. I'll help you break through your fear of selling so you can make the money you deserve and share your unique gift with the world. I'll show you how to effectively communicate your value and avoid the biggest mistakes that kill sales.

What you will learn

I'll walk you through EPIC ACT, a seven-step process I developed after 18 years in the trenches of selling and learning. When I began my sales career, the tool that helped me the most was a yellow sticky note on the side of my monitor with an acronym spelling out each step in the sales process. *How do you know if you're on track for a sale? What do you do next and when?* When panic set in, I would look at that sticky note to help me stay on track.

I created EPIC ACT to help you, entrepreneurs and freelancers, do what you love and get paid well for it. It's for people who want their life to be an "epic act". Staying motivated through the ups and downs of selling and dealing with rejection can be tough, so I begin with practical wisdom on how to stay the course.

These are tools and techniques I've used myself, so I know they work. And I promise you, these strategies will help you in all areas of life. You'll also learn practical tips and strategies to get your sales game on, so you will know how to meet a cold prospect and steer the relationship towards a successful sale, again and again.

What is selling?

Nothing happens until someone sells something.
- Thomas, J, Watson, former CEO of IBM

A sale is a mutually beneficial exchange of goods or services for money. In other words, selling is fundamentally about influence. But what is influence?

> Influence: the act or power of producing an effect without the use of force.
> Origin: influencia, in flow

Sales is about being in the flow.

When you're trying to move someone from A to B, you're getting them to take action, motivating them to make a decision, to buy from you.

Average salespeople, the people you and I come into contact with on a regular basis, try to push buyers from A to B. Excellence is about making B more attractive, making B more interesting, making B more valuable.

SALES = CREATING VALUE

In order to create value, you have to shift your thinking. Instead of acting from a place of selling (or pushing), try to act from a place of service (or giving).

SERVE, DON'T SELL

How people buy

Before moving on to the sales process, first you need to understand how people buy.

Need ⟶ Research ⟶ BUY ⟶ After sales service

It starts with a need. You broke your phone screen so you need a new phone. Maybe you don't want a phone that shatters when a feather lands on it so you decide to try something new. You'll look at different websites and reviews and then test them out. Then you'll buy. You want to make sure you made the correct decision so if you're not happy or anything breaks, you want to be able to exercise your money back guarantee.

The same approach applies if you're hiring someone. After reading this book, you may grow your sales so that you need more staff to help you. Your research entails posting jobs and interviewing candidates. Then you'll hire someone. The probation period is a kind of after-sales guarantee.

It always starts with a need. What they (the clients) need, not you needing to sell your stuff. Bad salespeople get it the wrong way around, approaching sales as needing to sell their stuff. People only buy because they have implicit or explicit needs and they perceive value in what you have to offer. Sometimes when you meet clients they don't realise they have a need until you show it to them.

In the next chapter I will begin walking you through the seven-step sales process to help you successfully sell and get paid for doing what you love, without turning into one of those desperate salespeople. Let's go!

STEP 1: ETHOS

The way we think about our life diminishes or enlarges the control we have over it.

- Martin Seligman

Sales is about your customer but it starts with you. Why? Because how you think affects how you feel, which affects what you say and how you act, which determine the results you get. Your thoughts are cause and the results are the effects.

Why this matters

Think about how many times you regret saying something because you were in a grumpy or angry mood. Have you ever made a passive aggressive comment to your spouse, kids or colleague? What was the response? Contrast that with the reaction you would get had you spoken from a happy or positive state. It's different, right? It's the difference between your kid throwing a tantrum and going to sleep. Or between hitting a project deadline and missing it. This is why Ethos is the first step in the seven-step process.

What does this have to do with sales?

As a freelancer or entrepreneur running your own business, your product may be unproven. You've probably quit your job to courageously take a path untrodden. Operating from the space of lack, limitation and competition will affect your performance during client calls and meetings. No amount of technique can help you in that state.

Sales is a game where for every ten prospect calls you make, nine will reject you. And for every five prospects that express interest, maybe one will eventually lead to a sale. Simply put, you will face a tonne of rejection.

Dealing with rejection is especially challenging if you're prone to pessimistic thoughts, as I used to be. You might have to deal with this even more if your product is brand new. Therefore, how you manage your state is critically important to ensuring every client touchpoint is the best it can be, increasing rather than decreasing your chances of landing a sale.

Dumping baggage on your clients

One time I worked with a startup co-founder called Stephen who had left an illustrious career with a big management consulting firm. During one meeting, he blew down the would-be clients like a hair dryer, barely letting them get a word in edgewise. He missed how the prospect's eyes glazed over. He didn't notice that he interrupted the prospects every time they spoke. And he failed to ask questions to learn more about them.

You see, earlier that day, Stephen met with a potential investor for the startup. And right before the client meeting, he was on the phone with a solicitor, angrily negotiating the close of a new house. Oh yes, and after work, he had a meeting with a wedding planner to discuss his nuptials for the following year.

Stephen thought he went into that meeting with nothing more than his laptop and phone. Little did he know he'd dragged in three big suitcases of worries with him and dumped them all over the potential clients around the table.

He wasn't at all "present", which negatively affected his performance. Distracted - unconsciously or not - by the need to "get" investment and income, he acted in desperation, throwing away a potential sale.

Unwanted company

The problem lies with that voice incessantly chattering in your head. The voice that starts talking when we wake up in the morning, telling us about a conversation we had yesterday, what we need to do tomorrow, thoughts about next week, how incompetent we are, or how we're not good enough. That voice constantly swings from past to future, stuck in autopilot. In other words, it is not in the present.

We'll quickly explore how the brain works to better understand how to manage your state so you don't turn into one of those desperate and annoying salespeople.

How your brain works

Have you heard the claim that you only use 5% of your brain's capacity? Well, it's sort of true. The prefrontal cortex is the part of our brain responsible for conscious thinking and it's the last major region of the brain to develop in the span of human evolution. According to neuroscientist and mindfulness expert Daniel Siegel, our prefrontal region is responsible for the following functions[1]: self-regulation, attuned communication / empathy, emotional balance, response flexibility, fear modulation, decision-making, recall, moral awareness and intuition. Basically, it sets goals, controls impulses and solves problems.

While it deals with a lot of functions, it also has major limitations. I love David Rock's analogy about the brain's limits on processing resources in his book *Your Brain at Work*[2]:

> Imagine the processing resources for holding thoughts in your mind were equivalent to the value of the coins

in your pocket or purse right now. If this were so, the processing power of the rest of your brain would be roughly the size of the entire US economy (before 2008).

When you become driven by survival, something that happens to sellers when they desperately want to close a sale to solve their cash-flow concerns, Daniel Siegel[3] says you lose most of those nine prefrontal functions, regressing to primitive behaviours. In other words, you lose the ability to balance emotions, leaving flexibility and compassion behind. This is the problem Stephen was having; he was driven by survival, so his brain literally didn't have access to empathy.

When you're in fear-driven survival mode, you lose your ability to have cognitive control, i.e. control over your mind, a necessary prerequisite to gaining access to insight[4]. People who have more insights are those who have greater awareness of their own thinking, and can therefore change how they think. When you can change how you think, you can change how you feel and what you say.

Now that you know this, what do you do? Don't worry, in the next chapter you'll learn how to override your mind's counterproductive tendencies so you can operate at your full potential.

Being Present: How to avoid being a typical salesperson

Realise deeply that the present moment is all you ever have.

- Eckhart Tolle

The first pillar of Ethos - an empowered mindset to sell without being salesy - is Being Present.

Think about the last time you washed the dishes or walked to the train station. I love Jon Kabat-Zinn's (Professor of Medicine at the University of Massachusetts and creator of Mindfulness Based Stress Reduction) quote: "Next time you're taking a shower, check to see if you're actually in the shower or are you having your Monday morning meeting in there too?"

My partner and I joke about the shower being the evil zone because I'd go in there in a good mood and return feeling angry or anxious, looking totally distracted. It's because while showering I ruminated over past or future events. Now that I'm aware of this, I make a conscious effort to remember where I am.

According to Daniel Siegel[5], studies from UCLA show that naming an emotion effectively soothes it; in other words, naming is taming. This works because awareness enhances neuroplasticity, the brain's ability to change itself. Siegel says, "awareness is the scalpel we can use to resculpt neural pathways"[6]. This means that you can break the habit of incessant thinking by being aware of your thoughts. It took me a while, but I learned to do this.

Siegel defines mindfulness as a "form of mental activity that trains the mind to become aware of awareness itself, to pay attention to one's own intention [...] and to observe the present without judgement"[7].

Dr. Sara Lazard, a prominent neuroscientist, extensively studied the effects of meditation and yoga on brain activity and structure. She used neuroimaging, fMRI snapshots of the brain[8], to examine their impacts over an eight-week period. She scanned the brain before and after the eight weeks and detected a thickening of the prefrontal cortex area, the part of the brain that looks after our conscious activities.

What does this all mean? Exercising your mind to be aware and practising mindfulness helps increase self-control, keeping your emotions from running wild and reducing the chances of becoming desperate and pushy. You can achieve greater empathy to become better attuned to prospects needs, improve your recall to ask better questions and tame fears so they don't hijack meetings.

In my Mindful Sales Masterclass, I provide a number of techniques to help you become more present. For now, I'll share one effective technique I learned from Eckhart Tolle[9], author of the best-selling books *The Power of Now* and *A New Earth: Awakening to Your Life's Purpose*.

Use your common sense!

This technique is about using your sense perceptions to become aware of your surroundings. You can begin by listening to the sounds around you. What can you hear? Right now I can hear the wind rustling the leaves, birds tweeting, the faint sound of traffic and the hum of a plane in the distance. What can you hear around you? Make a note of as many sounds as you can hear right now in this moment.

You can also become present by paying attention to what you physically feel. Right now I can feel the chair I'm sitting on, the cold keyboard beneath my hands and the plastic keys beneath my fingers. Next time you're traveling somewhere, be aware of what you're touching, how your feet touch the ground as you walk, or the sensation of your hands in your pockets.

You might be thinking, "okay, now what?"

There's nothing else to do. Presence is a state of *being*, not *doing*. When you become aware of your surroundings, you come out of your head, which is focused on the past and future, and enter the present moment.

At first it's difficult. Thoughts run wild. But the more you practise, the better you will become. The key is to not judge yourself or become annoyed when those thoughts arise. Just watch the thoughts and name them. Naming is taming.

For example, I'm at my desk, I can feel the keys under my fingers, my feet touching the floor. Suddenly, I remember I must email Immy about that workshop. I don't get annoyed, I just tell myself that's a thought about a workshop.

That's it. It's extraordinarily simple and yet really difficult, at first. Imagine you have decided to take up running. You don't run ten kilometres on your first attempt unless you want to be sore and frustrated. You begin slowly. Perhaps you run one kilometre every day for the first week, then two the following, and so on.

So now you know a simple way to get yourself into the right state to avoid turning into a desperate salesperson. Next, you need to know how to stay driven, but without that typically abrasive aggression of a salesperson.

Your Purpose: Unlock your most powerful source of motivation

Those who have a why to live can bare almost any how.

- Viktor Frankl

The second pillar of Ethos is to remember your purpose, your "why".

According to *The Power of Full Engagement*[10], written by Tony Schwartz, your spiritual energy is the most powerful source of human motivation, perseverance and direction. Spiritual energy is about having a deeper connection; serving something beyond our own interests ignites a deeper sense of purpose. When we focus solely on ourselves, we drain our energy but focussing on a purpose greater than us gives life meaning. And this purpose is a powerful source of motivation.

Purpose creates a destination.

- Tony Schwartz

Remembering your purpose and being mindful of why you started your own business helps you stay focussed. It takes attention and stress away from you so you can focus on making a positive impact.

As an entrepreneur or freelancer, you have a distinct advantage over salespeople in corporate environments. When you immerse yourself in your purpose, your "why", and operate from purpose instead of a need to close the sale, your energy will be different. You'll come across authentic and passionate, two beautiful and contagious character traits. Humans have an innate desire to do good and be a part of something bigger than themselves.

Imagine watching a movie with bad actors. You'd change the channel, right? A typical salesperson who uses canned techniques comes across like a bad actor. Buyers can feel this and change channels. When you tap into your higher purpose, to serve the world with your gift, to be part of a movement, people will feel your passion and authenticity and the effective sales techniques I'll walk you through later will come across naturally.

Where it all begins

Do you remember a time visiting a retail store where the shop sales assistants asked if they could help you? Remember how you felt? Did it feel like they really wanted to help you or were they asking because they wanted to get their commission? Maybe they're not conscious of it but buyers can sniff out the seller's intention a mile away.

In a workshop, a freelancer once asked, "I heal people with my hands, so how do I get over this feeling that I'm using this process to manipulate people, to make them vulnerable, to make them scared to then try and get them to say 'yes'? Isn't it just manipulative to use this process?"

Everything begins with an intention. Is her intention to manipulate people, to make them vulnerable so they give her their money? Or is it to heal them so they can live happier, pain-free lives? If it's the former, then that is the energy prospects will feel and it will likely push them away. But if it's the latter, the freelancer will draw upon compassion to help the customer.

Take the field of criminal law as an example of the power of intention. Most crimes require proof of *intention*. Here is a passage in the standard textbook of every judge's *vade mecum*[11].

> When the law requires that something must be proved to have been done with a particular intent, it means this: a man intends the consequences of his voluntary act, (a) when he desires it to happen, whether or not he foresees that it probably will happen; and (b) when he foresees that it will probably happen, whether he desires it or not. Intent or intention involves the existence of a state of mind comprising the decision at least to attempt to achieve the intended result.

All acts begins with the intent to achieve a result, whether or not it actually happens. Set your intention, be clear what you plan to achieve and then let it go.

Practise: Let your subconscious do the heavy lifting

95% of what we do is through habit.

- Tony Schwartz

Motivation, willpower and passion are awesome energies to get you moving, but they eventually run out of steam. The good news is you've got far greater resources you can mobilise to help you become superhuman. Those resources are your daily practises, your habits. We are creatures of habit. It should be no surprise then that the third pillar of Ethos is practise, using daily practises to set your mindset up for success.

Cast your memory back to the first time you sat behind the driving wheel of a car. Remember all those pedals, the gears, the mirrors? There were so many things to do, some at the same time, and you had to keep your eyes on the road. If you don't drive, think of the first few times you had to use public transport in a new city.

Now, you can probably drive singing along with the radio,

drinking coffee and chatting on the phone. Have you ever found yourself reaching your destination and not remembering how you got there?

The first time you sit in a car to drive requires a lot of conscious thinking; your pre-frontal cortex is in overdrive. But repetition carves out new neural pathways in your brain, pushing the new driving skills into your subconscious and freeing up space in your prefrontal cortex. This explains why after a while, we can drink coffee, chat, and sing to music while driving, and then forget how we got to our destination!

This example demonstrates the power of developing empowering subconscious practises to help us get through some of the challenges with sales and running our own business. Prospecting (i.e. generating new prospects) can be a boring and not particularly enjoyable task, but it's a critical part of your sales activity. You won't make sales unless you get new leads. Furthermore, the way you deal with setbacks is a habitual behaviour. Sales is about wading through the rejection to get the "yes".

In my Mindful Sales Masterclass I teach four powerful techniques to help entrepreneurs and freelancers confidently sell without being that annoying salesperson. But right now I want to share with you one technique that I learned that helps me stop my mind from spinning out of control.

How to shift from negative to positive

The mind is a wonderful servant, but a terrible master.

- Robin Sharma

Even the best salespeople get rejected on a daily basis and frequently, multiple times in a row. It's easy for people to get discouraged. But once you get discouraged, it becomes harder and harder to take more rejection. It takes more effort to make the next call. The phone feels heavier. You waste time faffing instead of getting on the phone or going to meetings. Before you know it, you're in a downward spiral. But if you carry on making 15 effective calls a day, unfazed by rejection, you will succeed

Psychologist Martin Seligman spent his life researching helplessness and optimism. His studies found resilience is not a quality you're born with; it can be learned. Being hopeful is the single most important factor, and whether or not you are hopeful depends on your explanatory style.

According to Seligman[12], your explanatory style determines whether you're crushed by defeat or rise to the occasion. There are three factors to look out for in your explanatory style: whether you believe setbacks are permanent or temporary; whether you make them personal or external; and whether you view setbacks as pervasive or isolated.

Say you had a client meeting and for whatever reason, it didn't go as well as you had hoped. After the meeting a voice in your head says, "I always mess things up, I'll never get this business off the ground, my life is ruined!"

Using words like "always" and "never" suggests the situation is permanent. The idea that one single meeting will affect the whole business or your life is another symptom of pessimism. These kinds of statements, your explanatory style, can paralyse you into a state of inaction and helplessness. If this is what you tell yourself, then what kind of feelings and actions will follow? If you tell yourself everything is ruined or that you always mess up, what's the point of carrying on?

If you have the tendency to dwell on the negative, don't worry. You can develop more optimistic thought patterns. The first step is to be aware of your thoughts as you learned in the first stride, Being Present. When you notice you're thinking negatively, you can do something about it. Here are two approaches Seligman[13] suggests:

Distract

Distract yourself by thinking of something else.

1. Out loud, say "stop" while clicking fingers.
2. Pick up an object and study it with all of your senses. This works because you can only think of one thing at a time.

Redirect

Once you've distracted yourself and created a gap in the negative chatter, you can redirect the thoughts by using one of the following techniques:

1. **Proof**: Show it's factually incorrect. For example, if there was a typo on a proposal and that voice in your head tells you you always mess up, dispute it by reminding that voice it's not true. It's only on the odd occasion you make a mistake.
2. **Swap:** Most events have many causes. Pessimists latch onto the worst cause, the permanent, pervasive and personal one. Ask yourself what's good about the situation or a more constructive way of looking at it. Focus on changeable, specific and non-personal causes.
3. **Helpful:** Ask yourself, "How is thinking about this helping me solve it? What's a better question to ask? What's good about this situation?"

A startup founder I was coaching was terrified of selling. He was passionate about helping graduates find meaningful work but he had to sell to corporates. The trouble was, he hated corporates. But they were the ones who would pay the bills so if he didn't get over this block, his thoughts, words and actions would repel them.

In one coaching session, we used the *swap* and *helpful* techniques to begin replacing negative thoughts with productive and empowering thoughts about corporates. Focussing on how corporates served his higher purpose and helped fulfil his mission made him more comfortable selling to them.

When you begin practising some of these techniques to

handle "no" effectively, you'll be able to take them on the chin, and power on to get to "yes".

Now that you know simple techniques to help you manage your state, you'll learn the five mindsets critical to sales success. Read on, they might not be what you think.

Nanakorobi yaoki (fall down seven times and get up eight).

- Japanese proverb

Cultivate a successful seller mindset

Nothing can dim the light which shines from within.

— Maya Angelou

In my workshops, participants often ask what it takes to successfully sell. Most entrepreneurs I meet worry they don't fit the right personality traits to successfully sell; they're not smooth-talkers, oozing confidence.

After 18 years of selling and researching the experts, I know that sales is an inner-game. If you don't have belief in yourself, then no sophisticated techniques will help you. Ever. I've tried and it doesn't work. So I'll share with you five mindsets important to successfully sell.

Continuous improvement is a way of life

Knowledge is power…and it will help you serve and earn more. As Jim Rohn says, "If you change, everything will change for you, when you get better, everything will get better for you. To have more you have to become more."

I wouldn't be where I am today if I hadn't developed a

voracious appetite to learn and improve. I used to be so scared of public speaking that an audience of just four people would paralyse me. It started with the first time I was interviewed for a podcast. After the one-hour podcast on a topic in my area of expertise, they couldn't patch together two minutes of content! I could barely string a sentence together. The interviewer repeated questions several times to help me answer in a coherent manner, but I just couldn't do it.

After that incident I vowed to learn public speaking so it would never hold me back again. At the time, I was a little lost in my career. But I found a new passion in public speaking. As a result, I can now serve more people. Mihaly Csikszentmihalyi[14] said, "those who don't continue to learn are not free [...] because their thinking will be directed by other's opinions, mass media. They will be at the mercy of experts." So nourish your mind with continuous learning and improvement.

What you have is valuable and can help others

You could learn all the sophisticated sales techniques from the most accomplished sellers in the world, but they don't make an ounce of difference if you lack absolute belief in your value and the benefit you bring to others.

In my sales career, I've always performed well when I believed what I was doing was of value to others. A lifetime ago, I moved to another country for a new job. A few weeks after packing up everything and moving to another continent, I realised the job wasn't at all what was advertised. The product didn't meet the quality and specifications we were marketing to customers and I just couldn't bring myself to be passionate about something that wasn't what it seemed. After four months of struggling to sell a product I didn't believe in, I failed and was sacked.

I soon found another job selling a product I knew delivered value and I was able to create new income streams.

What is a belief?

A belief is an emotionalised state of mind. "Motion creates emotion," said Tony Robbins, the world-renowned high-performance expert. New beliefs can be created with new thoughts, but new thoughts have to be charged with emotion or feelings to give it *motion*. Emotion gives a new thought the traction to become a belief. Affirmations are one tool to create new beliefs, but they are only effective when you believe in them, otherwise they create a greater gap between where you are and where you want to be. The best way to develop new empowering beliefs is by giving thoughts or affirmations momentum, and you can do this by thinking about your purpose.

Never let your small business make you small-minded

I love this quote from Brendon Burchard[15]: "Never let your small business make you small-minded." It perfectly sums up how entrepreneurs and startups feel when they first strike out on their own. A fashion startup I worked with was concerned about the small range of merchandise it offered compared to its competitor. I reminded her that Ralph Lauren started with just a few pairs of socks. That didn't stop him from approaching a big brand retail store to let him have space, which he got it. What matters is that it's a perfectly crafted range.

When my partner and I launched our own magazine, we needed great editorial to attract readers and revenue, but as a self-funded startup we didn't have the budget to pay for esteemed writers, so we had to be creative. We approached the vice-president of a major African nation for an interview and we got it. We landed an interview with an Afghan Minister for a salient issue affecting the industry. We won funding from a major foundation. We achieved all of this even though our magazine was unheard of!

World sprint champions don't cross the line by looking at their feet; they finish by keeping their eyes firmly on the finish line, running as fast as their legs can carry them. So think not about where you are, but about where you're going. Let your vision, your purpose, your mission of where you are headed, propel you.

Always be curious

Begin to cultivate an interest in people; wonder what makes them tick, marvel at their accomplishments, watch them light up while talking about their dreams, goals and ambitions. Empathise with their challenges and resolve to explore the ways you can help them.

When you develop curiosity about people - instead of talking or pitching - you can't help but ask questions and let them talk first. Instead of waiting for your turn to talk or waiting so you can respond, you can't help but listen fully. Instead of hogging the spotlight, you shine the spotlight on them.

When you are deeply curious about discovering, instead of trying to get what you want, you can't help but understand what is of value to people. Always be curious of people because when you give them your attention first, you are more likely to gain theirs.

How can I serve them and help them get what they want?

Zig Ziglar said, "You will get all you want in life, if you

help enough other people get what they want." This is such a powerful truth because as I said before, people pay for value. Sales professionals get a bad rap because most care only about taking, hitting targets to earn their commission. They're very me-focussed.

When you develop a focus on helping others get what they want, you will always create value. People pay for value and when you bring them value, they will want to buy from you, collaborate with you, and refer business to you.

Before moving on to the next step of the process, I want to touch upon a topic that strikes fear and insecurity in people.

How to stop letting competition make you feel insecure

Thinking about competitors can make you feel threatened, driving you into survival mode. It can sometimes set you off on that downward spiral of doubt and despair. Here's some knowledge that helped me deal with competition.

The word "compete" derives from two terms in Latin; "com" and "petere", which mean "together" and "to seek, to strive", respectively. Most people seek to actualise their potential and this task is made easier when others force them to do their best.

In his classic book on developing the highest levels of performance *The Inner Game of Tennis*, Timothy Galloway[16] explains how competitors help you achieve new levels of excellence: "By playing the role of your enemy they become your friend. Only by competing with you do they cooperate. It's the competitor's duty to create obstacles for you, just as you do for them."

By striving to do your best, you give each other the opportunity to find and push the limits of your potential.

Andre Agassi, the former world number one tennis player and grand slam winner, recounts his final tennis match before retirement in his autobiography *Open*[17]: "I turn and see Baghdatis extending his hand, his face says, We did that. I reach out, take his hand, and we remain this way, holding hands, as the TV flickers with scenes of our savage battle."

It was a punishing match that left both players in agony. Agassi recalls that final match as some of the best tennis he'd ever played. Commentators called it a classic.

However, there is a caveat. In his book *Flow*[18], psychologist Mihaly Csikszentmihalyi claims competition improves performance only as long your attention is focussed on doing the work better. In other words, if you focus on impressing others or winning a major contract, then competition becomes a distraction to inflate your ego rather than an incentive to focus your consciousness on what you're doing.

True competition is like true cooperation. Each player tries his hardest to defeat the other, but it isn't the other person he is defeating; he's simply overcoming obstacles presented by the other to become the best he can be. The greater the challenge and obstacles you face, the greater the opportunity for you to discover your true potential. It's only your deepest challenges that draw out your greatest effort.

The energy that it takes to look back and see where the other guys are takes energy away from you. And if they're too close, it scares you. Don't waste your time in the race looking back to see where the other guy is or what the other guy is doing. It's not about the other guy. It's about what you can do. You just need to run that race as hard as you can. You need to give it everything you've got, all the time, for yourself.

- Oprah Winfrey

True empowerment

Remember, sales is about your customer but it starts with you. In addition to learning various techniques and strategies, you need to understand people to succeed in sales. You're dealing with people's interpretations, emotions, egos and motivations, so in order to understand people, you have to put your own ego aside, otherwise you'll get swept away by their story or grievances. By being present and detached from any outcome, you can really serve them.

True empowerment comes from taking absolute responsibility for everything that happens to you. Why?

When you blame others for anything and everything, you give away your power. A freelance holistic therapist asked, "How do I communicate my value? People don't get the value in what I deliver, they just think it's a luxury one-off thing, they don't understand it requires ongoing treatment to be effective." The reason they think it's a luxury is because of the way they've been conditioned, the way they've been educated. They don't know any better. So there were two ways to approach this; either blame buyers for a lost sale, which leaves the seller powerless, bitter and client-less, or give up being right and take control by helping the buyers make more informed decisions.

If a client doesn't understand your product or service benefits, it's because you didn't communicate it effectively enough, not because they're stupid…no matter how much you want to believe that! And as discussed earlier in the section on developing optimism, don't make their reasons for not buying your product a personal attack on you.

To summarise, sales is about your customer but it starts with you because how you think affects how you feel, what you say and the results you get. Your thoughts are cause and the effects are the results you get. This is why Ethos is crucial; it underpins everything you'll learn in the next steps.

Now that you know how to manage your state to avoid being that annoying salesperson, you'll learn how to get yourself ready to execute your game-plan in the next chapter.

STEP 2: PREPARATION

Success depends upon previous preparation, and without such preparation there is sure to be failure.

- Confucius

Elite performers spend significantly more time training and practicing than they do in live events and competition. They understand the importance of preparation to success. There are four pillars in Preparation: Productivity, Physiology, Planning, and Proficiency.

The first pillar, Productivity, addresses a major factor contributing to poor sales and missing sales targets.

Productivity: How to spend more time where it matters

How wonderful it is that nobody need wait a single moment before starting to improve the world.

— Anne Frank

A major reason entrepreneurs and freelancers don't generate enough sales is not investing enough time developing new business or meeting prospects. You have to think of prospecting as an investment of time as opposed to spending time. It's an investment that will achieve the biggest return. A common reason for a lack of prospecting time is poor productivity and time management. So the first pillar of preparation is productivity.

If your business is new, you should be spending at least four hours a day on prospecting activities or handling existing customers. This assumes you don't yet have a business development or salesperson helping you.

Here are seven productivity tips to help you invest one

more hour a day prospecting. That adds up to an extra 31 working days a year in front of prospects. If you invest an extra month on your prospecting activities, you will grow your sales.

1. Only Handle It Once

How often do you read an email, text message or tweet and don't respond until later in the day or later in the week? I'm guessing it happens several times a day. On average, you will waste fifteen minutes daily revisiting opened correspondence. That adds up to around eight full working days a year. If you invested that time in front of prospects, I promise you would grow your sales.

To stop you wasting those precious weeks on avoidable stuff, here's a simple solution: Only Handle it Once or OHIO.

When you receive an email, you can usually tell by the sender and title whether it will need some thought before you can respond. If that's the case, don't open it. But if you think you can send a quick response, do it there and then.

Opening a message only to revisit it later not only wastes your physical time, it also occupies precious head space in our pre-frontal cortex. Whatever was in that message will follow you around, constantly tapping you on the shoulder until you respond. This seemingly harmless undercurrent of mind activity diminishes our brain's ability to operate powerfully and creatively.

Only handling it once frees your mind to operate faster.

2. Be proactive instead of reactive

What's the first thing you do in the morning after you wake

up? According to an IDC Smartphone usage study[19], you probably check your phone. Tweets, email, Facebook, Instagram, you name it.

In his book *Your Brain at Work*[20], David Rock says prioritising is one of the most energy sapping activities for the brain. Decision-making is another heavy mental activity, which explains the phenomenon of decision fatigue.

As you scan down your phone screen at your preferred social media site, each single item represents a decision to read or ignore, like or dislike. For each email and message, it's a decision to swipe and delete or open and read.

In ten minutes of email, media, and social media consumption, you've already made hundreds of decisions, each one firing off energy in the brain. It dumbs you down, starting your descent into decision fatigue. By the time you're at your desk to get some work done, your brain is already a little tired and distracted.

Here's how to access more creativity and energy. Restrict email and media consumption to certain parts of the day. Self-regulation, stopping yourself from doing something, also requires mental exertion. Eliminate the temptation of those flashing symbols telling you you've got a new message by switching off your wifi.

I tried an experiment where I switched from my smartphone to a dumbphone for four days. I couldn't read my email on my phone anymore or see who liked my Instagram photos. I scheduled a half hour at 11am, 3pm and 5pm to check email, read and do social media marketing. I did all of my creative work first and those days were remarkably productive.

Do your most creative and important work first, then check email and social media later in the day. Try it for just one day. See how you feel and measure your productivity.

3. Sprint instead of marathon

Set a time limit when you work on a task. When I sat down to write this book, I scheduled one hour a day. I would set my timer for 45 minutes, switch off the wifi so I couldn't get distracted and write for 45 minutes solid. The stopwatch created a slight pressure to perform.

When I went on to the next task, like writing the syllabus for a workshop, I set the timer for 45 minutes and did the same. And so on. Set a time limit and just go. You'll be amazed how much you get done in 45 minutes without distractions. After 45 minutes of focussed solid work, get up and stretch your legs for five minutes, then come back for the next sprint.

4. Three before ten

Do your three most important tasks of the day before 10am. Some say do 11 things before 11. I prefer focussing on quality instead of quantity. I tried the 11 before 11 and while I got stuff done, they weren't the most important things.

So pick the three most important things and do them before 10am. It might be writing a proposal, investing an hour on prospecting (obviously you'll do more later) or following up with clients. These are usually the money-making tasks.

5. Get ahead

Plan your work day in advance. Do this at the end of your working day, not in the evening when you're about to go to sleep, unless you *want* to stay awake.

I've tried a lot of time management techniques but the one that worked best for me is one from Chet Holme's book, *Ultimate Sales Machine*[21]. Here's how to manage your time in four simple steps:

Step 1: Priorities

At the end of your working day, list the six most important things you need to get done tomorrow. For example:

1. Work on that proposal
2. Email Arun
3. Email invoice
4. Write chapter in book
5. Write blog post
6. Review script

It's critical to make sure each item on this list is achievable in an allocated time. If it's part of a larger project, like revamping a website, or creating an email campaign, break down the bigger project into small manageable tasks. Then work backwards from the finished project date and chunk time slots according to what needs to be done along the way. Then simply list what needs to be done first.

Step 2: Duration

After writing your list, write down how much time you will allocate for each task.

1. Write chapter in book: 55 mins
2. Prospecting: 120 mins
3. Email invoice: 15 mins
4. Work on that proposal: 45 mins
5. Write blog post: 55 mins

6. Review script: 75 minutes

My list adds up to around six and a half hours.

Step 3: Prioritise

Prioritise the tasks in order of importance. Do the most difficult thing first. Complete tasks in descending order of difficulty so as the day passes, tasks get easier and easier. People typically want to do the easiest task first. If you leave tough tasks until the end of the day, you'll be lethargic and won't be as effective or you'll give in to the temptation to put it off until tomorrow. So do the hard stuff first and simply doing it first will give you a remarkable sense of achievement.

Step 4: Diarise

The next step is to schedule tasks into your calendar.

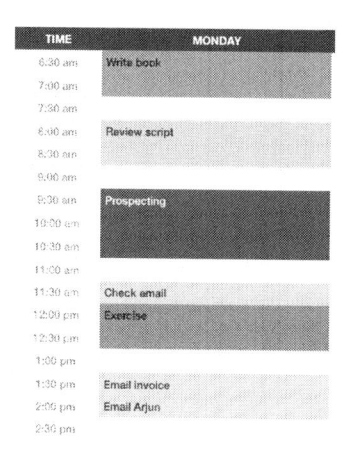

TIME	MONDAY
6:30 am	Write book
7:00 am	
7:30 am	
8:00 am	Review script
8:30 am	
9:00 am	
9:30 am	Prospecting
10:00 am	
10:30 am	
11:00 am	
11:30 am	Check email
12:00 pm	Exercise
12:30 pm	
1:00 pm	
1:30 pm	Email invoice
2:00 pm	Email Arjun
2:30 pm	

You'll notice there are gaps in the schedule. Don't make my mistake, which was to schedule everything back-to-back. This didn't leave time for breaks or to handle ad hoc items that needed my immediate attention. As a result, I went off the rails and didn't follow it. It works if you give yourself gaps in between and stick to it with rigid discipline.

6. Eliminate distractions

Switching between tasks expends valuable energy. When you're distracted from a task, it's like being yanked out of a deep sleep and can take you up to 20 minutes to get back into a focussed state again. According to Daniel Levitin, author of *Organised Mind*[22], it takes more energy to shift from task to task than it does to focus only on one, and when you focus on just one task instead of multi-tasking, you feel less tired after. So when you're working on a task, close down all distractions, unplug your wifi, face your phone down and shut the door. Kick the cat out.

7. Outsource

Outsource mundane repetitive tasks. I outsource my lead sourcing and searches for speaking opportunities. A virtual PA shortlists a number of suitable events and provides the phone number and email address of the correct people to contact. Doing this saves me over 10 hours a month.

If you're not spending at least two or three hours a day on the phone or with prospects, you'll never make the money you want.

So now that you've freed up time to invest in prospecting activities, you'll want to ensure those extra hours have the biggest impact possible. You don't want to waste the opportunity you've created for yourself. Head on over to the next chapter where you'll learn a simple and basic, but often over-looked part of high-performance sales.

Physiology: Simple tips to perform at your peak

To keep the body in good health is a duty, otherwise we shall not be able to keep our mind strong and clear.

- Buddha

Maintaining our energy is vital to performing at our peak. So in Physiology, the second pillar of Preparation, you'll learn two simple ways to help you perform at your peak when you're in front of prospects.

Why it matters

Around 4pm, towards the end of the working day, how you feel makes the difference between picking up the phone one more time to call another client or leaving it. It makes the difference between asking one more question to the client when you're on the phone or giving up. When you're in a 5pm meeting with a prospect, it's the difference between listening intently or launching into a rehearsed pitch.

It makes a difference in how you sound. Are you deflated and uninterested or energised and enthusiastic? When you're physically fatigued your patience wears thin, focus wanes and creativity plummets.

There are two ways to manage your energy: from the outside through exercise and from the inside, through diet.

Outside

When I launched the Middle East edition of *Forbes* magazine, I worked eleven-hour days, regularly giving seven back-to-back pitch meetings a day for weeks. If I didn't do my 6am swim every morning, there's no way I would have had the energy to run at full throttle for a sustained period.

Now, I do a number of speaking engagements and that takes a lot of energy, so I always ensure I get a solid sprint of exercise on the day of the event. It makes a world of difference in how I engage with the audience.

I'm not suggesting you become a gym rat, but it's important to recognise that exercise helps you continually operate at your peak, sustaining the flow that enables you to keep up with your passion.

Our rhythms

Sleep researcher Nathan Kleitman discovered humans sleep in cycles of 90 to 120 minutes. You move from light sleep, where dreaming occurs, into deep sleep, where your body's deepest restoration takes place.

This applies to your daily rhythms as well, according to

Tony Schwartz[23], author of *The Power of Full Engagement*. It's called your *basic rest activity cycle*. Your bodies crave sways in activity, from exerting and expending energy to resting and recovery. These sways occur in cycles of 90 to 120 minutes.

If you don't give yourself sufficient rest, you deprive yourself of energy and prevent your body from removing built-up toxins, making you susceptible to negative emotions, like stress, anger and impatience, and illness that will put you out of commission.

ROI of exercise

For every minute you exercise, you gain two to five minutes of productive time. Assuming you exercise 15 minutes daily, you're swapping 15 minutes of unproductive time for at least 30 minutes of very productive time. Conservatively, that's a gain of 15 minutes, a pretty good ROI of time and energy.

Rotating one minute bursts of high energy exercise with two minutes of reduced effort is more effective than long sustained exercise, according to Schwartz's research on interval training[24]. After reading this, I changed up my running with remarkable effect. I actually work out less than before and feel more energised.

Inside

What we eat affects our energy levels, too. You really are what you eat.

My partner is interested in nutrition, so we've tried many different diets, fasts and cleanses. Before meeting her, I just ate cornflakes and curry all the time! I didn't realise the importance of diet. The Paleo diet had the single biggest impact on my energy. After cutting out sugar and processed foods from our diet for one month, I dropped two sizes and my skin glowed. I felt energised throughout the day. No more 11am or 3pm dips, just a constant state of energy.

I'm no longer on the Paleo diet but have maintained many aspects like drastically reducing sugary foods, eliminating processed food and eating foods with a low glycemic index for breakfast. That's food that releases energy slowly rather than creating spikes in glucose (blood sugar). When you eat too much sugar, insulin swipes it away, stores the excess as fat, and suddenly you're left with a dip in energy. Then, you snack on junk to replenish your energy. Doing this just stuffs more fat into your cells and perpetuates the rollercoaster of energy spikes and dips. You'll find a link in the bibliography for the glycemic index of the 100 most common foods[25].

Do you want to spread passion for your product or circulate apathy? When you're physically fatigued you become impatient and lethargic. Selling from that state makes you ineffective and uninspiring. Your energy is contagious, so taking care of your physical energy through exercise and diet is of vital importance.

Now that you know the importance of your physical energy to selling more effectively, you'll learn how to achieve your sales goals. What do you have to do to achieve your financial goals? What do successful salespeople do to surpass targets? What is your blueprint for success? We'll cover all of this in the next chapter.

Planning: Where you're going and how you'll get there

If you fail to plan, you are planning to fail.

- Benjamin Franklin

It is critical to take a step back to look at the bigger picture, plot where you are and decide where you want to go. Humans are goal-driven creatures; it's how our brains are wired. Think of a goal as your pole star. Whenever you find yourself lost in the thick of it, you can look up and see where you are in relation to the guiding star and adjust course accordingly. Otherwise, you'll be lost at sea, unsure of what to do next.

Planning is the third pillar of Preparation. I'll walk you through preparing your sales plan and provide tips on face-to-face lead generation strategies.

What is what?

Before moving forward, here are a few terms I often get

asked to clarify.

Marketing vs Sales

Marketing is about raising your brand's profile with execution conducted through media outlets, i.e. it is one-to-many. Sales is how you grow the revenue and it's face-to-face, one-to-one.

Sales strategy

A sales strategy defines what you want to achieve. Three broad questions your strategy should answer are:

1. What are you doing now to grow your sales?
2. Where are the opportunities for sales growth?
3. Where do you want to be?

Sales tactics

Sales tactics are how you will execute the strategy. They are the actions that get the job done. Three broad questions your sales tactics should address are:

1. What will you do on a day-to-day basis to achieve your goals? E.g. attend four networking events a month and invest two hours a day on cold calling.
2. How will you build relationships and rapport?
3. Which sales channels will you use?

Sales process

The sales process is a series of predictable steps you have to take to sell your product and achieve your objectives. The idea is to eliminate uncertainties and create a repeatable and scaleable process.

Qualified prospects and leads

Before a customer becomes a customer, she is a qualified prospect - she has expressed interest in your product. Before she's a qualified prospect, she's a lead, a company or an individual that you've identified as a potential client.

We'll now move on to creating your sales plan. It's important to be flexible and adapt it to your customer's buying process. Be prepared to change your plans to accommodate what your customers want and your tactics to their style and processes.

Create a winning sales plan in seven steps

Give me six hours to chop down a tree and I will spend the first four sharpening the axe.

- Abraham Lincoln

1. Set your SMART goals

Get your free fill-in-the-blank sales plan template from www.mindfulsalestraining.net/book-resources

First you need to create a target, an aim. If you don't, you won't know if you've succeeded or not. In a sales plan, a goal can be a revenue target - a number or a percentage growth - or a number of new client acquisitions. It depends on your business plan.

One startup I worked with was focussed on the volume of clients rather than revenue because the founders were seeking investors. But another startup founder was focussed on sustainability without the intention of seeking external funding. She preferred revenue over number of clients as her primary target.

Your SMART goals must be:

- Specific
- Measurable
- Achievable
- Realistic
- Time-sensitive

2. Strategy: How will you achieve these goals?

There are five ways to grow sales:

- Up-sell or cross-sell existing clients
- Ask for referrals
- Build joint ventures and partnerships; develop relationships with resellers
- Develop new business
- Renewals

Examples of strategies might be:

- Up-sell seven customers to buy higher-priced product in Q4
- Recruit two resellers in Q3
- In September, launch a referral campaign

Now it's your turn. Make a list of your short, medium and long-term strategies.

Complete the sentences below.

1. My strategy for this month is…
2. My strategy for this quarter is…
3. In twelve months I will achieve…

3. Who do you serve?

Who is your customer? Is it a specific sector? A demographic? I'm assuming you've already done some market research for your business plan (there are plenty of online resources to help you write your business plan), so you should already have a clear idea of your ideal customer.

Complete the sentences below.

1. Our typical customer is.…
2. Their job title is…
3. They're aged between…
4. They tend to read the following media…

4. Competitor analysis

In order to articulate to customers how you are uniquely positioned to serve them, you need to conduct a competitor analysis. This involves comparing customer bases and competitive advantages.

Complete the sentences below:

1. What makes us distinct from others is…
2. When my customers think of me I want them to think…
3. People should buy my product because it helps them…

4. My product helps my customers achieve the following positive outcomes in their business or life…
5. I know my product can help customers get results because…
6. The reason they should pay the asking price is…
7. For people to pay the asking price they must feel…

5. Budget

What financial resources do you need to meet your sales objectives? Make a list of those resources you need to fulfil selling activities like events, travel or presentation materials. It's important to track the cost of acquiring new leads, both in time and money, so you can focus on the most efficient strategies.

I joined a business referral membership network which required a block of three hours of my time every week. After five months, I could count on my hand the number of leads I received. One day, I skipped a meeting and invested those three hours in cold calling. In those three hours alone, I secured meetings with several organisations giving me reach to potentially hundreds of target customers. I achieved a greater return on my investment (in time and money) by cold calling than attending the weekly meetings, so I terminated my membership.

6. Tactics: How will you reach new customers?

Tactics are the daily and weekly activities you perform to achieve your sales strategy. In this section, you should state how you intend to achieve your sales strategy. Example

>   Strategy: Develop network in the community

Tactic: Attend three trade shows this quarter, join five Linkedin groups this month

To help you prepare your sales tactics, complete the sentences below.

1. The media my customers read are ….[list the magazines, websites, papers, etc. that they consume]
2. The monthly and annual events my target customers attend are….
3. My customers also buy products and services:….[list similar but non-competing products or services]
4. My customers are represented by the following trade associations….[list organisations]
5. My customers are likely to be members of….[list organisations]

When you know where your prospective customers hang out, you can begin thinking about how you will reach them. I will share with you popular lead generation strategies in the next chapter.

7. How will you measure success?

What gets measured gets improved.

- Robin Sharma

There are two things you can measure:

- **Activities:** These are the things you do to achieve your goal. This could be the number of calls you make in a day, the time spent making calls or the number of events you attend monthly.

- **Results:** Obviously this covers what is actually achieved: revenue, number of new clients, number of meetings with decision makers, number of new leads generated, etc.

Activities alone don't really tell you much. When I started out in sales, I had a daily activity target of 20 effective calls, a call that lasted two minutes. Our calls were monitored by randomly checking our phone records. Often, I'd close a sale within two minutes, which meant it didn't count as an effective call. And by four in the afternoon, colleagues would spend about ten minutes calling fax machines to hit their quota.

Fortunately, you can't call fax machines now but you get what I mean! And as the business owner, you wouldn't do such a thing, but the point is to measure something sensible. Investing three solid hours on prospecting every day would be one example.

I suggest measuring both activity and results. Early on in your business, emphasis should be on activities because results take time. But when you perform the activities, you should eventually get the results.

Examples of sales metrics:

- Number of quality calls per day
- Number of quality face-to-face meetings per month
- New revenue vs renewals

Which sales activities will you measure? Complete the sentences below.

1. On a daily basis I will do these activities….
2. On a daily basis I will measure these results…
3. On a weekly basis I will do these activities…
4. On a weekly basis I will measure these results…

5. On a monthly basis I will do these activities....
6. On a monthly basis I will measure these results...

The purpose of this chapter was to give you a big-picture view of how you will achieve your goals, as well as zeroing in on the day-to-day activities you will do to get more customers and increase your profit.

The next section is where the rubber meets the road; it's how you go out and attract the customers to generate revenue. Before you move on, make sure you work through the exercises in this chapter.

The entrepreneur's money magnet

The force is strong with this one.

- Darth Vader

In this chapter I'll share with you effective in-person business-to-business (B2B) lead generation strategies. Since this book is about face-to-face selling, I will explain strategies involving in-person interaction in depth and summarise the rest.

1. Referrals

Getting referrals is the number one source of leads because it's baked with social proof. When someone gives you a referral for a plumber or a dentist, you'll probably employ them over a stranger you find in the telephone book or internet. Referrals aren't guaranteed business but they are warm leads. You get referrals by asking your clients and network to reach out to their contacts.

Training your army of salespeople

I cannot stress this enough: you have got to make it really easy for people to refer you. Here's how.

According to *Endless Referrals*[26], author Bob Burg suggests you first help your network identify a good referral. This means explaining to your friends and acquaintances the *benefits* of your product or service. This advice assumes you know the person really well and they're happy to refer business to you. It won't work with strangers.

Instead of stating your occupation, explain the value people get from your services. So instead of telling them you're a web designer, tell them you show startups how to present a sharp brand image so they can attract customers. The latter is much more compelling, right?

After explaining how you serve, you'll have to tell them how to identify a good prospect for you. You could say, "I could be of help if a startup mentions they need to make their website mobile friendly, or they need to refresh their website."

Finally, you need to *ask* for the referral. Be specific, e.g. "Do you know someone who has recently started their own business? Great, do you feel any of them would be open to learning more about…?"

For more on developing referrals, I highly recommend reading Bob Burg's book.

2. Cold calling

For B2B selling, cold calling is the second most powerful and effective lead generation strategy. You might have heard that cold calling is dead. *Bad* cold calling is dead.

Intelligent cold calling turns your phone into an ATM machine.

You probably hate cold calling. Perhaps you get multiple cold calls a day. They're awful and I hate them too. But the ones we get are intrusive consumer cold calls, they're not calling about your business. "Hello Ma'am, I'm calling about your car accident last week." I didn't have an accident last week. I don't even have a car.

How to cold call intelligently

Cold calling for business is different. If you can *legitimately* help businesses be more profitable or help them get what they want, then it's your duty to give them the opportunity to thrive.

It's also your responsibility to communicate it in such a way that informs them how you add value. So you need to have empathy, not sympathy. Sympathy stops you from calling them, empathy gives you understanding. Your desire to help them has to be stronger than your fear of disturbing them.

My Conscious Cold Calling programme is a step-by-step deep dive into how to effectively cold call, developed from my 18 years of success. The core of the teachings is this: you need to focus on *them* and how you can help *them*. More often than not, sellers mistakenly start talking about themselves and the product. They use the telephone as though they're fruit sellers walking down London's Oxford Street shouting, "Come get your delicious apples, come and get your ripe bananas, we sell oranges, apples and bananas, come and get your ripe bananas!" That might work for Oxford Street to people casually shopping on a weekend, but it doesn't work for busy executives operating under the pressure of deadlines and targets.

The ability to call someone you've never spoken to before, stoke their interest in something and create a desire to meet to potentially buy from you is a powerful skill to develop.

3. Email

Email is great because you can reach a large number of people, quickly. It's less effective than cold calling because you're relying on the recipient of the email to act and respond. How can you be sure the email didn't end up in the spam box? Did they read it or not? Who knows?

If you rely solely on emails and follow up only to those who respond, you're missing out on prospects. How many times have you opened an email with the intention of following up, but it ultimately drifted lower down your priority list? I'm guilty! But when someone follows up, I'm on it.

Cold emailing tips that work

On my Conscious Cold Calling programme, I teach how to write emails that get a response. Right now, I'll share three things that determine whether someone opens your email: the sender, the subject-line and the first sentence. These are the first things people see in their inbox. In a split second, the recipient will decide to delete or open your email (assuming they see the email in the first place!).

Sender

Make sure it's a real person's name and not a generic spammy address, like, hello@hotcompany.com or info@newcompany.com.

Subject

Make it benefit-focussed. Ask yourself, "Why should they care? What's in it for them?" "Helping you attract more leads" is one example of a benefit-focussed subject line.

Email body

- Keep it short.
- If you have a referral, lead with that. If not, start with something personal.
- Begin with your benefit statement, or how you add value, not your job title.
- Do not forget the call to action, e.g. suggesting meeting dates.

There's no fixed approach that works 100% of the time because you're reaching out to individuals. Maybe they've had a bad day or they've been in back-to-back meetings. You never know. But following these tips will increase your success rate.

4. Partnerships

Partnerships include resellers and organisations, and they can be a remarkably speedy way to multiply your reach and revenue.

Someone once approached me on Twitter to promote her workshop to my readers. In return, she offered to give me 25% of the proceeds of each seat sold. Since I already knew plenty of excellent providers of the service she offered and could not verify her experience or credibility, I decided not to proceed. I did not want to risk upsetting my readers, who I work so hard to look after. However, had I been able to verify that she was an excellent service provider and that she was aligned with my mission to help folks like you prosper, then I absolutely would have agreed to her partnership proposal.

On another occasion, I identified a partner I could work with who's mission was aligned with mine. I reached out, offering a free workshop for her audience. Her audience derived a lot of value from that workshop. After, I asked the potential partner if she would be interested in helping more of her clients while earning revenue, proposing a 50% revenue share for each seat sold of my online class. She said, "just let me know when". It's a win-win.

First, identify non-competing companies or organisations who serve the same customer as you do. Thoroughly research their organisation and the management. Reach out to them offering to help them. Think about how you will incentivise them to sell your products. If you're just after leads and not sales, then think about what the partner will get out of it. Typically they want to add value to their customers, so maybe you could offer a freebie to their customers. No one will just give you their customer list because their reputation is at stake. You have to add value first and make it really attractive for them to share.

5. Networking

Talk to someone about themselves and they'll listen for hours.

- Dale Carnegie

There's a common misconception that in order to be a good salesperson that wins people over, you have to be a smooth talker or the life of the party.

This is total rubbish. I used to network with investment

bankers. But my indifference to the topic of finance and introverted tendencies didn't prevent me from having effective interactions with prospects. After a 20-minute conversation with a senior banker at one networking event, I made my excuses so I could move on to others. "Well I really enjoyed our conversation, it was great chatting with you, thank you," he said with a beaming smile. I just asked four questions. He did *all* of the talking.

People like talking about themselves more than anything else in the world. Let them talk and just listen. And I mean really listen. Most people are just waiting to talk, listening to reply instead of listening to understand. Also, let the other person feel like the smartest person in the room; don't try to one-up them and prove how smart you are, which is what most people do.

The key to being a magnetic networker is to shine the light on others rather than hogging the limelight. That's how you light up a room.

3 great questions to ask

1. "What's exciting for you right now?"

This question gives people license to talk about anything, not just work-related topics. Maybe they're about to go on holiday, one of their kids graduated from school or they're working on an exciting new project. Let them pick the subject and let them talk.

Don't interrupt and talk about a similar experience. Don't let your mind wonder about what to ask next. Just be in the moment, listen and ask follow-up questions.

One time I asked this question to a prospect in a meeting. She talked so enthusiastically about an exciting new project and 15 minutes later she said, "Oh no, obviously don't tell anyone. You're going to have to sign an NDA, now."

2. "What's challenging for you right now?"

Again, this question gives the respondent license to talk about anything.

You should ask these questions in the order presented here. Question one opens them up by getting them to talk about their favourite subject. And it prepares them to talk about question two, a question not everyone is comfortable answering right off the bat. It appears too salesy if you ask question two straight away.

3. "Who would be an ideal referral for you?"

If they haven't started talking about their job already, then ask them about it. How long they've been doing it? What do they like about it? A question that will set you apart is, "I'm just wondering, who would be an ideal referral for you?"

A good follow-up question to that is, "what question can I ask them to find out?" Asking anyone how you can give them more business will make you memorable.

Your primary objective should be to give. You do that by searching for ways you can help them. Remember Ethos, your intention is to serve them. Networking events aren't an opportunity to pitch, they're opportunities to meet people and find out how you can help them. Each person you meet knows at least 100 people, so when you enter a room and there are 50 people in there, it's really 5,000 people to which you're gaining access.

Don't be one of those people who is going for numbers; focus on quality connections and focus on the long-game.

How to follow up to keep the ball rolling

If you have a good referral in mind, send the introduction the next day. They should respond by thanking you at which point you can suggest meeting for a coffee to explore if there are other areas where you could be of service.

During coffee it should be quite clear you're expected to talk more about business. By now, provided your email signature had your website and social media links, they most certainly will have researched you and your company so it should be unnecessary to send you bio or explain what you do.

Instead of pushing, you're attracting.

6. Events

Events rank highly on the effectiveness scale because of how quickly you can meet and qualify leads. It's worth taking time to look for events your prospects might attend. If you're a competent speaker, approach organisers for speaking opportunities to add value to their audiences.

If you're hosting a stand at an event, focus on gathering leads instead of trying to directly sell to them. They've probably been bombarded by hundreds of people trying to push products down their throats already. Think of the lifetime value of a customer instead of trying to go in for the kill right away.

7. Webinars

A webinar is like a live meeting or presentation on the internet where you can give demos, share your screen and get audience participation. They're a great way to attract large engaged audiences. They're interactive, as opposed to passive like video. I've only run a few myself, so I'm not the right person to comment on this but there are plenty of great resources out there to run webinars. Check out software providers like Webex or WebinarJam, which also offer tips and advice on how to run successful webinars.

8. SEO

The SEO landscape is changing all the time, and it largely has to do with how Google sets its algorithms. What makes for successful SEO as I write this just might change again by the time you read this book. At the moment, content is king. Great content, often-searched keywords and inbound links from other popular websites pointing to your website help enormously. I'm not an expert at all on this so do your research to find out what works for you.

9. Advertising / Sponsorship

This includes online advertising like banner ads, Google Adwords, Facebook and Linkedin. At the moment, Facebook ads give you bigger bang for buck in terms of audience reach. For B2B, the best advertising is to give away a valuable free report so people join your mailing list. When they join your mailing list, you continue adding value with content. Other advertising mediums include magazines, radio, podcasts, public transport spaces and billboards. For events sponsorship, identify relevant industry events, then approach organisers with ideas for the value you can give attendees.

10. Blogging

Also known as inbound marketing, blogging is a great way to establish authority and credibility. It's a brilliant way for you to level the playing field with larger competitors. Besides setting up your own blog, also consider avenues like Medium, Tumblr and Wordpress where massive audiences already exist. Just remember to always point posts back to your company website.

For more on how to blog for your business, Copyblogger is a great resource.

11. Public Relations (PR)

PR is about appearing in other media. Being interviewed on websites or podcasts and getting write-ups or reviews are a few examples. Contributing articles and blog posts also works.

12. Social Media

For B2B lead generation, social media ranks the poorest in terms of effectiveness, so use your time wisely. However, it is worth being active. According to Gary Vaynerchuk, brands typically mistreat social media as a distribution channel. Instead, use them as story-telling channels. Linkedin and Facebook are the best social media outlets for B2B.

Think about how you'd work a room in real life and do the same on social media. Give value first, instead of pushing your product. To get the best out of Facebook and Twitter, read *Jab, Jab, Jab, Right Hook* by Gary Vaynurchuk. The people at Linkedin publish plenty of information to get the best out of the Linkedin platform.

From all of these lead generation strategies, you have to pick what's right for you. It's best to mix them up, test, measure and tweak as you go along. Whatever you do, don't just rely on one strategy.

Proficiency: How to punch above your weight

Not all readers are leaders, but all leaders are readers.

- Harry S Truman

Authority is one of the most powerful triggers of influence[27], according to persuasion expert and author of Influence: The Psychology of Persuasion, Robert Cialdini. If someone tells you to do something, you're more likely to listen to someone in a uniform, like a policeman or a judge, than a random person on the street. Authority as a persuasion trigger works with knowledge and credentials, too. As a relative newcomer, your proficiency could level the playing field with your competitors. So here's the fourth and final pillar of the preparation step: Proficiency.

There are two key areas to pay attention to: product knowledge and industry knowledge.

Product knowledge

Given that you're passionate about what you do, product knowledge should be relatively easy for you to master. You're probably already working on this so I won't dwell. Work on your expertise, develop your skills and hone your product. Know the latest trends, innovations and debates in your specialty. What skills can you learn to become better at your craft? Remember, continuous improvement is one of the traits for sales excellence.

Industry knowledge

Positioning yourself as an expert is a powerful way to build authority in your market and, therefore, a powerful trigger of influence according to Robert Cialdini[28]. Be a student of your industry and the industry of the people you serve.

If you want decision makers to see you as a peer, you have to meet them at their level to have strategic conversations with them. You have to add value for them and their business and help them meet their objectives. So you need to understand their market and you can achieve this by being aware of the economic, social, political, technological and environmental drivers that impact their business performance.

Conversations with customers are some of the best learning opportunities. That's how I developed my knowledge of emerging markets when I sold to investment bankers and government officials.

I knew absolutely nothing about banking and finance. After doing my own research and developing enough knowledge to ask intelligent questions, I learned a lot from prospects and clients. I borrowed opinions and perspectives from one client, expressed them to another, and learned from the experts the different viewpoints. That made me look like an expert.

But - and there's a big but - just because you've done a little research or you've read one article, don't profess to be an expert to clients by talking about all the facts you read. I've seen this time and time again. This is the ego's need to feel important. Remember to come from a place of service; use the little information you've learned as a way to show understanding by asking intelligent questions that achieve a deeper understanding.

Crucially, you need a thorough grasp of how your product helps prospects add value to their market, their industry. It's pointless just learning about their industry, which is relatively easy. Your value is positioning yourself to help them add value to their industry with your product.

With patience and persistence, eventually you'll develop a well-rounded view of the industry which clients value.

Complete the sentences below.

1. The websites I can subscribe to learn more about the industry I'm in and serve are…
2. The books I can buy today to learn more about the industry I'm in are…
3. The biggest trends affecting my client's industry are….

Two skills to learn

Learning the two skills below will help you quickly become an expert.

Speed-reading

Most people average about 250 words per minute. If you're

like most people, the only time you were trained to read was when you *first* learned to read. You were told to sound out each letter, and read one word at a time. That was the extent of your education. That's why most people read slowly.

You can train yourself to take in more words at a time, or broaden your "visual gulp" as Tony Buzan calls it in *The Speed Reading Book*[29]. After practising, I increased my speed-reading from 250 to 850 words per minute, and can race through 300 page books in days instead of weeks.

This book isn't about speed-reading but there are plenty of resources out there to help you. I liked Tony Buzan's book because he gives you exercises after each chapter to broaden your visual gulp. My reading speed accelerated within a week.

Rapid learning

Another great skill to have is being able to pick things up quickly. Just like any other skill, it is something you can learn and develop. I scored an E in my English GCSE, which is basically a fail, and had to resit a school year. I managed to scrape by with a C, just enough to let me do A levels (high school for Americans). I managed to make it through my adult working life by writing bullet points. In sales, you don't need to write essays.

When I wrote my first essay in over 15 years, I asked my partner to take a look. She scribbled red pen all over it. She turned to me in dismay.

Partner:	Do you know how to construct a sentence?
Me:	What do you mean?
Partner:	You know, subject-verb-object?

I knew then, it was bad. Really bad.

I took online courses, read books and practised. Eighteen months later, my dissertation was published in an academic journal. Maintaining a strong appetite for learning attunes your brain to learn things quickly, positioning you to help serve more people.

Now that you've freed up more time to focus on revenue-making tasks, got your plan of action, understand the importance of maintaining peak physical state to be effective and see why being a master of your craft will help you, you're ready to move on to the next step.

What do you say to prospects when you're in front of them without being a typical annoying salesperson? How do you actually have a conversation with a prospect so that it turns into a sale? That's what we'll cover in the next step.

STEP 3: INVESTIGATION

First seek to understand before being understood.

- Steven Covey

Now that you have a plan, you've carved out time to focus on revenue-generating activities and you're looking after yourself to maintain momentum, let's orchestrate your interactions with prospects so it leads to a sale.

The biggest mistake people make when selling their products is showing up and talking about themselves. Sellers cannot wait, to start talking about themselves or their product; they want to pitch as soon as possible. There's a technical term for this: "showing up and throwing up".

This chapter will help you avoid this big mistake. You'll learn what to do and say when you're in front of prospects. First, I'll address your most powerful intrinsic sales tools to help you during the investigation step.

Two intrinsic sales tools to help you investigate

I've learned that people will forget what you said, people will forget what you did, but people will never forget how you made them feel.

- Maya Angelou

In networking or sales scenarios, most people don't listen, they're waiting to talk. They're listening to reply instead of listening to understand. If your mind is occupied with selling or circling the prospect like an eagle waiting for its prey to make a wrong turn, for her to say that one word that triggers you interrupting with how you can save the day, then you're not truly listening. And you're not serving. You're being self-serving. People can feel this.

1. Mindful listening

Your first tool is your ears.

Start by being present, being detached from any outcome

and free of judgement. Listen with the passionate intent of understanding so you can help them. Set the intention before your meeting to fully understand them so that you can help them. Your prospects will know you're there to help them because they can feel your intentions, which shapes your behaviour. They will talk to you as though they are talking to an old friend, telling you challenges they would be far too defensive to tell anyone else for fear of seeming weak.

In my workshops I always advise entrepreneurs to listen first and listen more than they talk. Someone once asked, "How do you show passion when you're listening or asking questions and not talking enthusiastically about your product?"

2. Passion is an inside job

Passion comes from the inside, not from the outside. When your client is doing all the talking, responding to your questions, the action you're taking is listening with the intent to understand.

In the classic book *The Seven Habits of Highly Effective People*, author Stephen Covey says the single most important principle in interpersonal relations is this: "Seek first to understand before being understood"[30]. This is especially important in sales. Interpersonal relationships are the foundation of successful selling.

Typical sales people just want to tell and sell. Telling ain't selling. It's annoying. People will respond not to what you say, but you make them feel.

The most influential conversation

80% of my conversations with others occur inside my head.

- *Your ecards*

When you first meet prospects, the most influential conversation isn't the one you're having with them. The most influential conversation is the one going on in their heads. It's their opinions, perceptions and concerns.

Psychiatrist Abraham Maslow[31], whose research on human motivation underpins most change management

```
              /\
             /  \
            /Self-\
           /actual-\
          / isation \
         /----------\
        / Self-esteem \
       /    needs      \
      /-----------------\
     / Social needs, love \
    /    and belonging     \
   /------------------------\
  /    Safety and security   \
 /----------------------------\
/      Physiological needs     \
--------------------------------
```

approaches over the last three decades, says that we are driven by a hierarchy of needs, shown on the previous page. When each need is met, we're motivated by the the next rung on the ladder.

Most people you meet are concerned with earning more money, achieving greater success, climbing the career ladder or looking good in front of their peers.

In a *Harvard Business Review* article on why self image matters in B2B sales and how it influences buying decisions[32], over 70 supplier attributes were surveyed. All things being equal, the three top attributes buyers value were:

1. Helping buyer meet their company objectives
2. Enhancing the buyer's productivity
3. Enhancing the buyer's self-worth

Humans are wired to take the path of least resistance. We want an easy life. We're living in the most information-saturated time in human history, with millions of messages vying for our attention on a daily basis. As the brain evolves, it's natural for us to seek the path of least resistance.

So the questions you need to ask yourself to get the attention of prospects are:

1. How can I help prospects meet their objectives?
2. How can I improve my prospect's productivity?
3. How can I make them feel good about themselves?

When you shift your intention from "how can I sell to them" to "how can I help them buy", you bypass the pushy salesperson stereotype. You attract instead of push.

How to ask questions

You can take a horse to water but you can't make them drink. But you can show them how thirsty they are.

- unknown

There are two types of questions to ask: open and closed. Open questions encourage people to answer in sentences so they are good for discovering more about the person and their business. Closed questions are those that can be answered with a single word or phrase. They're good for gently steering the conversation and getting a direct answer.

On my Mindful Sales Masterclass I share five powerful questioning techniques and show you how to create your own questions. Here, I want to share with you what I call the "4A" questions.

1. Affinity - Does the prospect like you? Do they trust and respect you?

2. Ambitions - What are they trying to accomplish this year? What do you think it would take to increase their business?
3. Aggravations - What frustrates them most?
4. Already - What have they already tried? What worked and what didn't?

1. Affinity

People do business with people they know, like and trust, so the first objective in the investigation process is to develop an affinity with the prospect. Adding value is a given. When you meet someone in person, the first step is to build rapport. This basically means creating harmony and making the other person feel comfortable with you. When you do that, you inspire trust, respect and confidence in you.

How to build rapport

I know some people hate small talk. They don't get it.

But here's the thing, small talk doesn't have to be about you talking. It can be about getting the other person to talk. Small talk is a way of building rapport, warming up the other person before diving into their deeper issues.

The key to successful rapport-building is to always be curious about people. There's a timeless saying in selling: "Always Be Closing". If "Always Be Curious" were the primary dictum of sales, I bet there'd be far fewer annoying salespeople in the world.

On my Mindful Sales Masterclass, I take you on a deep dive into how to build rapport quickly to accelerate the sales process. But for now, I'll share with you questions you can ask to help you get to know the prospect.

A day in the life of…

To figure out your prospect's challenges and goals, you need to put yourself in his or her shoes.

Answer the questions below.

1. What do they do in their role?
2. How are they rewarded?
3. What is the definition of success to them?
4. Who do they report to?
5. What are they accountable for?
6. What are their passions?

To prepare an entrepreneur for her first meeting with a major new prospect, I listened to her initial cold call. The director had pulled a colleague onto the call at the last minute and it was obvious that the colleague was unhappy and uninvolved. After completing the *day in the life of* exercise, the entrepreneur realised the importance of engaging the disgruntled colleague as early as possible. It was clear the colleague felt she had no choice in attending the meeting so to satisfy her need for autonomy and reduce the barriers to a successful sale, engagement with this individual, early in the meeting, was critical.

2. Ambitions

Now that you've developed rapport, the next step in the journey to achieving a sale is finding out what the prospect wants. What are their goals? What do they want to achieve this year? Remember the Zig Ziglar quote: "You can have anything in life you want if you just help enough others get what they want."

At this stage you ask questions to find out what your clients want to achieve so you can help them get it. It is the foundation of successful selling.

Example questions

- What are your objectives for the year (or quarter)?
- Where do you see yourself in a year?

Now, write down a list of five questions you could ask prospects to learn more about their ambitions for the year.

3. Aggravations

Now that you know what your prospects want, the next step in the investigation stage is to find out their aggravations. Even if you already know some of their challenges, you want *them* to start talking about it. If you tell them, you'll come across as the stereotypical aggressive salesperson, making the prospect defensive and uncooperative. You ask questions to get *them* talking about their pain points instead of you talking and telling.

Here's an example from when I was selling to publishers. I asked a prospect two questions: "How is mobile affecting your business model?" and "Do you find more readers are browsing on mobile but your revenue model hasn't caught up?" She was very forthcoming. She spoke for the next 15 minutes about how they've outsourced certain functions and were losing 80% of their revenue.

Now, write down a list of ten questions you could ask that uncover their aggravations.

4. Already

Now that you've discovered your prospects' challenges, you want to find out what they've already tried doing to address it. What hasn't worked and why? You do this to get them in a solution-oriented frame of mind while determining how to position yourself differently from what they've already done.

Examples

- What have you done in the past to help alleviate this challenge?
- How have you addressed it in the past?

Now, write down a list of five questions you could ask prospects to learn about what they've tried doing to solve their aggravations.

No one will answer deep questions about challenges off the bat. You have to build up to it, to win permission to ask these questions. You achieve this by building affinity, trust and authority. Asking someone to talk about their ambitions, goals and vision gets them excited, opening them up. They start to feel comfortable answering questions about aggravations and challenges they're facing. Then you're ready to explore what they've tried, what worked and what hasn't, to learn more about how you can add value. Hold off talking about you and your services until later. Your time will come.

Now that you have your 4A questioning system, I'll show you techniques to avoid sounding typically salesy.

How to avoid sounding canned

When you're attached you're repelling; when you're detached you're compelling.

- Anis

People hate being sold to so when buyers detect typical canned sales techniques, their defences shoot up and you lose them.

If you're new to selling, you might feel a bit guilty selling to someone. If you feel guilty, it comes across in how you communicate. You will appear awkward. It's like watching a movie with bad actors; you can't stand it so you change the channel. When the acting is good, the actors aren't acting, they're being. With those films, the audience forgets about actors because they're so absorbed in the story.

Remember to be present

If you worry about being nosy or generally feel uncomfortable while asking prospects questions, it's a cue for you to get present. Take your attention out of your head and into your senses and your environment. Feel the chair you're sitting on, feel the table or your feet in your shoes. If you are listening to that internal dialogue, it means you can't hear what the other person is saying and you won't have access to your creativity. Focus on listening to the prospect.

Since you're meeting with someone, I'm assuming he or she is a qualified prospect. A qualified prospect is someone who 1) you can help with your product and 2) has shown interest. Set your intention before your meeting and then let it go. Don't cling to any outcome; be detached, otherwise you'll come across needy and desperate.

You will find there are times when you ask the same questions to different prospects. So how do you ask them without sounding canned?

The key to authenticity so you don't sound typically salesy

The key to authenticity is your intention.

If you deeply care about their well-being and how you can help them, you can't help but be authentic. When you immerse yourself in your purpose there's no room for guilt.

It's okay to plan questions; it shows you care and you've done your homework. To help me connect with my authentic self, here's what I ask myself before meetings, presentations and speaking engagements:

- How can I help them?
- How can I serve them?
- How can I help them get what they want?

I repeat it like a mantra to take attention away from me and my selfish needs (of wanting to be liked or getting it right) and focus on them. And it reminds me of my bigger "why", my purpose, which is to help others succeed. Our mind cannot focus on two things at once. When you're steeped in your purpose, the ego has no room to take hold.

Set a clear goal

Be clear to yourself about what you need to achieve for the interaction to progress further. Do you want them to agree to a trial? Agree to have a demo? Or do you want to get an introduction to other decision makers? Your objective is to progress the sale, which can be measured by action.

During new prospect meetings, talk to your prospects like you're talking to a friend. You'll find a lot of people in corporate jobs have this bubble around them. That's not the real them or the person across your kitchen table. I'm not talking about slurring your words but when you relax into your authentic self, you give them permission to do they same. They will eventually mirror your body language.

Here's a reminder of the "4A" questions.

1. Affinity - Do they like you?
2. Ambitions - What are they trying to accomplish this year? What do you think it would take to increase their business?
3. Aggravations - What frustrates them most?
4. Already - What have they already tried? What worked and what didn't?

You've developed rapport with your prospect. You know their ambitions, aggravations, and what they have tried so you can position yourself as a viable alternative. Now you should be ready to show them how you can help them.

STEP 4: CONFIRM

People may doubt what you say, but they will always believe what you do.

- Lewis Cass

This next step in the process is tiny but significant. People tend to put more faith in what they say than what a salesperson tells them. Your prospect's needs and desires are the foundation upon which you justify your price, your product, and the action you want them to take. Before talking about you and your product, you must establish a need or a challenge you can solve for them, demonstrate understanding, and get their agreement that there is a challenge. Also, you need to gently transition from the prospect talking about themselves to talking about you. The Confirm step achieves all of these elements.

Don't drop the ball

Once you've uncovered the prospect's challenges, needs and desires in the Investigation step, always always ALWAYS confirm those things to them.

It's like holding up a mirror. Confirmation shows that you paid attention and understand them. Doing so also achieves a tiny commitment. Small yeses lead to larger yeses. According to persuasion expert Robert Cialdini[33], this works because people have an innate desire to be consistent with what they say. So a small "yes" now may trigger a bigger "yes" later, to ensure the prospect is consistent with what he or she said before.

If you can't confirm challenges or objectives at this stage, you haven't established a *need, want or desire*. In other words, you haven't demonstrated how you can add value and therefore why they should pay you. You'll need to go back and do more investigation, otherwise you won't make a sale. Below are two examples of how you do this.

Example: Selling a survey software

> Just so I'm clear, you want to increase customer feedback so you can improve your service, you want to know where leads come from so you can focus your marketing effort to grow your sales funnel, and your biggest goal for the year is to grow your sales by 20%. Is that right?

Example: Selling a phone

> Have I got this right? You use your mobile for work, you use spreadsheets a lot, create presentations, and use the internet and email. You're not bothered about camera and other media like music, right?

After you get the nod, here are good follow-up questions inviting them to add to the list:

> Anything else you want to add?
> Is there anything else?
> Did I miss anything?

Another good follow-up question to ask at this stage:

> What else are you looking for in a new widget?

Asking this question gives your prospect the chance to tell you their explicit wants or their criteria for buying.

Before you launch into talking about you and your offer, here are great questions to ask to help you understand the buying process and who else is involved in the decision-making:

> Who else is involved in the this decision that you think I should meet?

> Is there anyone else you think I should meet that would benefit from a time-saving process?

If they mention their partner or colleague, you could reply:

> Tomek, if you're happy with how we can save you time in your supply chain, shall we fix a time to meet your colleague? Saves you the trouble of explaining it.

Saying it like this positions it as a benefit for Tomek, so he doesn't feel threatened. He probably has better things to do than giving a presentation to his colleague. Including the phrase "if you're happy" is a get out clause for him. There is no pressure on him and he retains has autonomy.

I used to make the mistake of not finding out about others involved in the buying process. When it came to the close, the prospect would say, "I need to discuss it with my colleague, it's not up to me." If they don't introduce you to their colleague, then focus on helping the person in front of you as much as you can. Help them sell it to their colleagues.

In the next chapter I'll explain when and how to start talking about you.

When to make it about you

Before talking about you, you need to pivot from them talking about their needs to you talking about how you can help them. You'll use the Confirm step as a way to achieve the transition.

Here's the setup:

> Just so I'm clear, you want to increase customer feedback so you can improve your service, you want to know where leads come from so you can focus your marketing effort to grow your sales funnel, and your biggest goal for the year is to grow your sales by 20%. Is that right?

And now the pivot:

> We helped Small Biz grow response rates from 2% to 48%, giving them rich data to stay ahead of competitors. I'll show you how we might be able to do the same for you.

In this example, I lead with how a similar company benefited from the service, a powerful tool for influencing. If you've got happy customers, mention them.

If you don't have existing happy customers, you could use this:

> So Mia, you're having problems locating suppliers and you want to double your sales, by working with resellers. Have I got that right?
>
> [Wait for agreement]
>
> We can help you track down the best suppliers. Let me show you how our widget can help you cut down recruitment time so you can start multiplying your revenue.

And that's how you pivot to talking about you in relation to what they need. It's how you set yourself up to demonstrate how you can add value.

Confirming and summarising their needs has multiple benefits. It shows you where you are in the process of the sale. If you can't confirm their needs and challenges and wants, it means you haven't uncovered them and you don't have a foundation for a sale. You haven't established a need to create value. People pay for value.

The prospect knows you're listening and you understand them. People believe what *they* say, not what *you* say, so repeating their words compels them to be consistent later in the process. Confirming is the perfect setup to pivot to your demonstration from them talking about themselves. This has to be carefully orchestrated, it's not a quick change of lanes. You look in the mirror, signal, then manoeuvre.

Now that you've laid the foundation for a successful sale, let's go on to the next chapter to start talking about you.

STEP 5: ADD VALUE

Price is what you pay. Value is what you get.

- Warren Buffet

You're on a roll now. You understand your prospect's ambitions and aggravations and you've elegantly transitioned from showing them you understand their challenges to how you can help them. This is the stage where you present your offer, which I call the Add Value step.

Just remember, always give your presentation *after* you've heard your prospect talk about their challenges and needs; you can only add value when you know what is of value.

How to talk about you and your product

1. Less is more

You might be tempted to talk about all the benefits of your product or service.

Don't.

After your meeting, your prospect will probably look at his phone on the way to his next meeting. Maybe he'll check Facebook, hit a few likes, share a funny Buzzfeed article, retweet something, tap a few images on Instagram, check email. Then he's on to another meeting. The prospect will eventually go home, perhaps to screaming kids, chat with his partner and switch on the Netflix to catch up on *House of Cards*.

There's a constant hive of activity demanding his attention, draining his energy. Your competitors are not just other people and companies in your sector.

You are competing with cat videos.

It's essential to make it as easy as possible for people to remember you and how you can make a difference in their world.

Less is more. The less you tell them the better. But what you say has to pack a punch. Only tell them benefits of your product that relate to a specific and urgent problem they brought up during the investigation period.

Example: Specialist recruitment agency

Saadia, you mentioned uncertainty leads to bad hiring decisions and it's costing your company around £25,000 a year, is that right? Let me show you how we could save you £25,000 a year by eliminating uncertainty in hiring. We carefully vet each candidate. They will have already completed a four-month internship with another company before you meet them. You'll get employees who have been trained to do the job you want them to do. So you will eliminate uncertainty in your hiring, reducing your risk of selecting the wrong person, saving you at least £25,000 a year, if not more.

Example: Financial magazine

So Kofi, since attracting investors is a key objective for you this year, you want to communicate to the international finance community how the policies you've enacted have made your country a fertile ground for generating competitive returns on investment? Let me show you how our platform helps you speak to emerging market investors when they're most receptive to your ideas.

2. Twitter-like benefits

People no longer have the attention span to read long paragraphs. They get lost in thought if you talk too much. Practice explaining the benefits of your offering in 140 characters or less.

Steve Jobs was a master presenter. His keynote speeches from product launches are legendary. In *Presentation Secrets of Steve Jobs*, Carmine Gallo[34] explains how Jobs used and *repeated* Twitter-like headlines loaded with benefits throughout his presentation. They were so powerfully crafted that the media used these same headlines to announce the launch.

iPod launch: "1,000 songs in your pocket"

MacBook Air launch: "The world's thinnest notebook"

Example for specialist recruitment agency: "Eliminate costly uncertainty by hiring people trained to do the job from day one."

Your turn. Turn each of your product benefits into a statement of less than 140 characters. Be sure to focus on the outcome, i.e. why it's good, and not on the feature.

3. If you can see it, say it

When I was selling to investment bankers for a niche publication, our competitors were *Financial Times* and *The Wall Street Journal*. To drive home our unique value, I would often say:

What would you prefer? To stand on stage to a sold out audience at Wembley stadium, where some but not all of the people in the audience are prospects? Or on stage at a sold out event at London's Brixton Academy, where every single person in the audience is a potential customer?

They would always choose the latter. Then I'd take it one step further and ask:

> So you're on stage to a sellout crowd at London's Brixton Academy. Everyone in the audience is your potential customer. In the front row you can see the Finance Minister and a World Bank official, over there you can see the Central Bank Governor. What do you want to say to them?

I used picture power, helping them visualise what it would be like to use our product as a medium to deliver their message. Doing so got them in the mindset of actually using our product and excited about the opportunity.

Imagine a scenario where your prospect is using your product. What would it be like? Now think about how you can help them walk into and around that picture. Think about the elements of your product you can use as a hook to get them talking.

Ask questions to lead them into thinking about how they could use your product or service. Where and how. You've got to help them get there by asking questions.

> Example: Selling to teachers
>
> How easy would it be for you to organise this activity? Imagine the kids were using these, how is it resonating with them? Are they excited? Imagine an OFSTED inspector sitting in the background watching all of this, how do you think they would react?

Not all these questions are relevant because it depends on what the prospect values. Some teachers will care just about the kids. Others will want to impress inspectors. You can gauge the right approach by how they answer some of your earlier questions.

4. Stories sell

Humans respond to story-telling. This builds upon the previous point about the power of pictures. One person attending my workshop sold beautiful, high-end food to local butchers. His story went like this:

> Imagine your customer Mrs.Santos coming in on a Sunday morning. She's looking for something new to cook for her in-laws who will be coming round later and you could offer her something new and handmade. Wouldn't she be pleased?

5. Repetition

Repetition boosts recall. Here's a simple structure for presenting your product:

- Tell them what you're going to tell them
- Tell them
- Tell them what you've told them

Example: Selling to teachers

You'll learn how you can boost your student's grades and keep OFSTED happy using our new simple tool. Here's how it works…..[explain benefits]
And that's how you could improve your student's grades and keep OFSTED happy.

The power of three is an effective and time-tested persuasion tool in speaking.

6. 4H

Sometimes you have less than five minutes to present your product and no time to answer questions. This usually happens when a bigger audience is involved. Here's a four-step process to help you deliver a persuasive pitch in 90 seconds or less:

Headline

Begin with an attention grabbing headline that states the benefit of your product or service. You do this by asking yourself, what positive outcome will your customers experience after buying your widget?

Headache

Next, explain the problem you're trying to solve or your target market's pain-point. To resonate with your customer, use the language they would use to define the problem.

Hangover

This is where you explain what could happen in the future if your target audience fails to take action. In a year's time, what might happen if they continue with the status quo? For example, if you're a plumber and your prospective client won't fix their leaking pipe, in a year's time they might need to change their floor boards.

Here's the solution

Finally, this is where you talk about how you solve the

problem with your product or service, followed by a call to action.

Random acts of value

No one has ever become poor by giving.

— Anne Frank

On my Mindful Sales Masterclass programme I teach you five powerful ways to add value, but right now I'll share a story of how I helped a prospect become a loyal customer.

I was selling to a Taiwanese chip manufacturer that wanted to enter the European market for the first time. After building rapport with the marketing director, I discovered some of her challenges: getting distributors and PR. She didn't know where to start.

Two weeks later, I called her and gave her the names, email addresses and phone numbers of the top ten distributors in each of her four target markets. She was blown away and deeply grateful for saving her time and money.

This information had nothing to do with what I was selling and it didn't cost me a penny. It cost me four phone calls and four emails to colleagues in four different countries. I leveraged my network to help my prospects.

Bear in mind, I'd developed relationships with those colleagues in advance. I gave them my time and understanding and in exchange, they gave me their trust. They knew I was there to help them. Otherwise, why should they go out of their way to help me?

I also helped the client get exposure to her target audience of over half a million people. I didn't give products away, I leveraged my network and invested a little time to help them in other ways. The client was grateful. Two months, later the client spent £60,000 with us, exclusively.

So what other ways can you add value to your prospects without giving your products away for free?

Complete the sentences below:

1. The lesson I learned about adding value to clients is…
2. Ways I can help my prospective clients without giving my products away for free are…
3. The daily actions I will take to add value to prospects are…

STEP 6: CONTRIBUTION

Only those who have learned the power of sincere and selfless contribution experience life's deepest joy: true fulfilment.

- Tony Robbins

This step of the process is tiny but significant. At this stage of the sales process, sellers get impatient because they're nearing the final stage, the dreaded close. They've presented their offer, sent a proposal and now they desperately want to get the business. Desperation creeps in. Remember, desperation is a deterrent. Taking action from a place of impatience, fear and desperation might not yield the best results. In all likelihood, you'll end up bugging the hell out of your prospects and scaring them off.

Imagine footballers taking a penalty shot. How often do they kick the ball outside the goalpost? Why does this happen? It's because they're so close to scoring, they're overwhelmed with pressure.

It's like a person poking you, repeatedly. Your instinct is to bat them away. It's annoying. Then you silence their calls and stop returning their emails.

How to avoid desperation

Only by giving are you able to receive more than you already have.

- Jim Rohn

Instead of thinking about closing, I invite you to focus on contribution. When you're eighty-five, sitting on a rocking chair and reflecting back on your life, closing that sale and making money probably won't be a key event that stands out. There is more abundance in the world today than there was thirty years ago yet the rate of depression is soaring. Happiness stems from living a meaningful life, not from money creation.

The questions that you will measure yourself against are: What are you giving? How are you making a difference in people's lives? Will I matter?

Asking yourself what you can do to help a prospect will shift you from annoying to serving. As you shift your intention from desperately trying to close to how can you contribute, serve and add value, how you think and feel will change and therefore how you act will be different.

To be clear, I'm not talking about giving your product and services away for free; there are other ways you can give. Every weekend I go to my local farmer's market (remember what I said about proper diet?). We were about to walk away from a stall when the man behind the counter said:

> Miss, those vegetables, you know most people throw the stems away and just cook the leaves. My grandma told me you can cook the stems, too. Chop them into two inch pieces, simmer them for one minute and you can cook them with the rest. Now you get two for the price of one.

We bought the vegetables. He didn't give us a free sample, he shared valuable information with us that didn't cost him a thing.

Instead of emailing the prospect with messages like "what are your thoughts?" and "tell me if you want to buy", you might say the following: "Hey, I came across this article about your clients and thought it might be of interest."

Instead of feeling annoyed and ignoring your email, they might say, "thanks, that's useful. By the way, just waiting for a few colleagues to return from travels before discussing your proposal with them."

Instead of being that annoying person, which I know you don't want to be, you can still be courteous and kind. And instead of bugging your clients and chasing them off, you can be the person who makes them feel good.

You want to strive to be this person even if the answer ends up being "no" because quite often, it will be. This will be an opportunity to learn how to overcome another objection or discover a way to improve either your offering or your pitch.

But if you start bugging them, they'll just ignore you to avoid the difficult conversation. So you have to be approachable regardless of the outcome. Maintain rapport to get the honest answer; maintain a relationship for the future and they're more likely to refer business to you. Be someone to whom they'd be happy to refer business.

To help you focus on contribution, go back to your purpose. What's your bigger purpose? Why are you doing this? How will this help people? When you focus on contribution while being detached from whether or not someone buys from you, you strengthen your trust with clients and pave the way for a robust, long-term relationship.

So now that you're focusing on helping prospects and you've taken the attention away from you, you're ready to move on to the next step. This is where you take action, where you help your clients make the decision to help them achieve their objective.

STEP 7: TAKE ACTION

It is literally true that you can succeed best and quickest by helping others to succeed.

– Napoleon Hill

The final step in the EPIC ACT process is helping your prospect Take Action to get what they want. Sellers get anxious at the closing stage. Fear of rejection kicks in and people feel awkward asking someone to buy from them. What should you say to seal the deal? "Have we got a deal?" or "Shall we do this deal?"

There's no need to use the word "deal" when you're closing. Maybe it's what they say in the movies but it comes across as over the top. Let's go over a couple of things you need to know about closing.

Techniques rarely speed up a sale

Pressure is more likely to be effective with smaller buying decisions (below £70) than with larger ones (anything over £100).

According to Huthwaite International's[35] research, experienced buyers don't like closing techniques. "It's the arrogant assumption that I'm stupid enough to be manipulated into buying through the use of tricks." And if you want an ongoing relationship with buyers, pressure tactics just make things awkward. Closing doesn't just mean getting the order; closing is getting a commitment.

If you're selling widgets that cost £50, closing the sale in one call is absolutely possible. But if you sell higher valued services that the person will want to consider further, fixing an appointment for a call or meeting in two weeks can be considered a close.

If the person suggests you meet with a colleague after that initial meeting, that too can be considered a close. The sale is progressing. Agreeing to trial your product for free is also progress.

Closing techniques do not make sales

People buy because of perceived value. You demonstrate value by showing how your product or service meets their needs and you can only do that by understanding their needs. So if you've skipped all the previous chapters and jumped straight to closing techniques, then I suggest you go back to the beginning.

There are loads of closing techniques. Over the many sales books I've read, I've counted at least forty techniques. As I've said before, less is more. It's best to become an expert at a few of them rather than attempting to learn all of them. Focus on the ones that resonate with you and your values.

I fear not the man who has practiced 10000 kicks once, but I fear the man who has practiced one kick 10000 times.

- Bruce Lee

These closing techniques I'm about to share with you only work when you understand your client's needs; they place value on how you could help them. Remember, the purpose of a close is simply to invite them to take action.

Closing techniques: Helping your prospect say "yes"

On my Mindful Sales Masterclass programme I teach the "ARTISTS" closes, that can help you close in many different scenarios. Right now, I'll share three simple classic closing techniques that have stood the test of time.

1. Assumptive

Let's start with an example you saw earlier:

> So you're on stage to a sold-out event at London's Brixton Academy. Everyone in the audience is a potential customer. In the front row you can see the Finance Minister and a World Bank official, over there you can see the Central Bank Governor. What would you want to say to them?

The close is right there:

What would you want to say to them?

By getting them to think about the content they'd like to deliver, I assumed we would do business together and that they would buy from me. The conversation continued:

Me:	Would you like us to write it with your help?
Prospect:	Our researcher can help.
Me:	So I will liaise with him?
Prospect:	Yes.

That was it. Simple, smooth, no fuss. It's my favourite close.

Here's an example of how one of my clients used the assumptive close. She asked, "How can I speed up and close them? Can I offer them a bundle discount? What else?"

I suggested she meet with them and talk about design aspects of the product she sold. She arranged a meeting with her prospect to show sample designs she'd created for them. During the meeting they talked about design and content. *All of this was effectively assumptive.* Later in the conversation, she asked when they wanted to start. They gave a specific start date. Sold.

More questions you could ask for an assumptive close include:

- Would your team need a demo when we've installed it?
- Who should I make the invoice payable to?
- When would you like to get started?

Variables you could use for an assumptive close are: start dates, points of contact, product variables or even the recipient of the invoice.

2. Trial

I call this the Aikido close. The key words to remember in this close are "if I" and "would you". Like the martial art Aikido, you use the person's force to follow through on the action. Typically, you will use what the client says to pivot into a close.

Imagine you're selling a tech product with customisation capabilities and the client says something that appears to be an objection.

Prospect:	Yes, but we need multiple users.
You:	How many do you need?
Prospect:	At least four.
You:	Anything else?
Prospect:	I'm not sure that the sharing capability will work for us. It's not quite right.
You:	*If I* could arrange for four users, *would you* be happy to move forward next week?

This trial close uncovers objections and flips them. You could also use date and time as variables for this close.

You could also use this close to test if the prospect is ready to close or to get an agreement before you even begin talking about your product.

Example of a trial close:

Before I begin, if I can show you how we can help you increase your revenue, would you be willing to begin a trial this month?

One caveat about this close. You have to solve the

problem, then follow up with the prospect. When you tell them the problem is solved, include the contract because you've already got the verbal agreement.

3. Select

Another classic close is to give the prospect two choices. Again, using variables like days and time or product and service details, you give them a sense of autonomy.

- Would you prefer the 3-month or 6-month plan?
- Do you prefer the one with 2 logos or 4?
- Would you like to meet on Thursday at 10am or Friday at 11?

Like the assumptive close, you should use similar variables. Avoid providing more than two options.

Did you notice I also included a meeting? To request meetings, it's best to use the select close over an assumptive close because you're making it easier for the other person to focus. If you leave it open, they have to decide on a date themselves, which requires more decision making and the chance they won't get back to you.

Your turn

Pick one of these closing techniques and think about how you can use it for your product. Some of them require bouncing off the prospect's answers. I find having an imaginary conversation about what a prospect typically says and how you can respond is a good place to start.

Rehearse it. Start building memory muscle so it's there when you need it. It's like when you first drive a car; there's the wing mirror, rear-mirror, gears, three pedals, roundabouts, reverse turns. So much to think about!

Yet by now you can probably drive while having a conversation, singing out loud or drinking coffee. You may reach your destination without realising how you got there because the act has become subconscious.

You need to practise these conversations so the technique lodges in your subconscious and flows out of you naturally. And contrary to what some people say, not all closing techniques are suitable for every situation. So pick one, learn it, then come back and learn another one.

How to avoid sounding "salesy"

You will find these closing techniques in sales books from the seventies. On paper they might look canned and clichéd, or some might say they're old fashioned. That doesn't change the fact that they still work.

But here's what separates you from typical salespeople using these very same techniques: when you're passionate about what you do and purposeful about helping your clients get what they want, what you say should resonate. What you're saying comes from a deeper, bigger place. Your motive isn't to manipulate the prospect into closing to win a commission. Your motive stems from love for what you do and a passion to serve others, an unparalleled force of nature. After learning and practising these simple techniques, you will naturally develop your own ways and words to close.

Now that you know simple ways to effortlessly ask for the sale, you should learn what to say when you get a "no".

What to do when a prospect says "no"

Dealing with rejection or objections is par for the course in sales. More prospects will say "no" than will say "yes". Not everyone is ready to buy when you want them to and not everyone will benefit from your services.

Sometimes a buyer needs your product but they've got a few unanswered questions preventing them from moving forward. In this case, it's the seller's responsibility to communicate the value. If the buyer doesn't fully understand, then it's the seller's fault for not helping them understand.

Why prospects say "no"

- They don't "get" the value of the product. This is often because you, the seller, launched into your spiel before uncovering the client's needs.

- They're not the decision maker. They might not have authority to buy so the process has stalled.

- They're confused. You may have spent more time talking about features and not enough time on benefits.

- Timing. Either the prospect signed up with another provider or there are internal issues they need to address.

- They doubt your capability. You haven't provided enough social proof or you lack self-belief.

- They doubt your credibility. Sufficient rapport, trust and authority hasn't been established, or you lack self-belief.

- The features are not quite right. You may have focussed on the wrong benefits during the presentation or didn't adequately qualify the prospect.

Handling objections

The best way to deal with objections is before they happen. I cover this topic in depth in the Mindful Sales Masterclass but right now I'll share with you a four-step process on how to handle them after they happen.

When the client raises an objection, the key is to first find out if there are any other reservations. Then lead the conversation to the value of the product.

A typical objection could involve a prospect comparing your services to those of an incumbent. Here we return to the example of someone selling survey software. They claim they can get more credits at lower prices with a competitor.

   1. **Validate them:** "I understand, you want to be sure the price you're paying is worth the quality, right? [Wait

for agreement]. I'd do exactly the same. Let's put price aside for a moment."

2. **Check for other objections:** "Apart from that, is there anything else?"

3. **Return to value:** "You mentioned you're planning new products later this year. Wouldn't having quality customer feedback be extremely important to get the product right the first time?" [Wait for response].

4. **Lead to benefit:** "How do you think our software's ability to generate customer response rates up to 45% higher than the market average would help inform your product development?"

The last question gets the prospect talking about how your product benefits them. If a prospect cannot articulate the value of your product at step four, it means you haven't sufficiently uncovered their needs and demonstrated how you can help them. In which case, you should consider returning to the Investigation step.

How to reduce price objections

Don't share the price too early in the process otherwise the prospects will be preoccupied with the number and they won't hear the value.

Now you might be thinking, "If they asked for the price, then surely we should give it to them?" Price is connected to perception, and we have the tendency to contrast it with what we've just experienced. If you give them the price off-the-bat, you haven't given them an opportunity to experience any perceived value to counterbalance it.

If I walked into a clothing store, stood at the front door and asked "How much?" before looking around, wouldn't that look a bit daft? I'm not calling your prospects daft but rather showing you that it's okay to postpone price conversations until after prospects understand the value of your offering.

Focus on value first. Get them wanting your product before mentioning price.

If they ask "how much" early on in the conversation, postpone the answer by saying, "Great to hear you're interested. I'll definitely give you the price, but right now I'm not even sure you have the problems we can solve." Then ask a question.

Or you could say, "Great to hear you're interested. I'll definitely give you the price. But to give an accurate quote I need to learn a bit more about you to determine the right solution." Then ask a question.

So next time a prospect says "no", don't panic. Use this four-step formula to turn things around or learn more about why they're objecting.

How to nurture prospects for the future

Not everyone is ready to buy. In this case, your objective is to nurture the prospect to keep the door open. You can achieve this by continuing to add value without giving your stuff away for free. Find reasons to get in touch with them to add value.

Complete the sentences below to guide you.

1. Five articles/blog posts I could write for my prospects are....
2. An idea I have for my customers I could share is....
3. These are the interesting topics I can go back to my prospects and talk about....
4. The ways I can add value to prospects without giving my products away for free are....

Your intention should be to continue serving and giving. One freelancer I know gets in touch every two months to ask if I want to hire him for anything. Now, whenever I see his email in my inbox it makes me squirm because I know he wants something from me. Remember, how you make people feel will affect whether or not they buy from you.

So avoid being that annoying mosquito. Instead, set the intention to delight your prospects on a regular basis.

ONWARDS AND UPWARDS

And will you succeed? Yes you will indeed! (98 and 3/4 percent guaranteed).

— Dr. Seuss

I hope you've found utility and value in these ideas to help you grow your sales so you can continue doing what you love.

Before I finish, let me share with you an a-ha moment I had years ago. I used to think I had to become a behavioural expert or learn lots of different personality types to become the best salesperson. But when I started my mindfulness journey, I realised you don't have to learn complex patterns and multiple buckets to characterise people.

You only have to know yourself.

One way takes years of study and has the unfortunate side effect of putting people in boxes. The other can be known in a heartbeat.

When you truly know yourself, you will know others because we are all connected. It's as simple as that. When you know yourself, you can rise above your ego's selfish needs. When you rise above the ego, you won't get sucked into people's dramas, or jolted by quirky personalities. The desire to judge that gets in the way of the sales process and rapport and connection will slowly fall away.

Let me share one last example from a Friday cold call.

Prospect:	Dave Richards speaking.
Me:	Hi, Anis here from *Development Post*. Good time, bad time?
Prospect:	It depends why you're calling.
Me:	We help companies like yours engage stakeholders, so I called to find out if we might be able to help you.
Prospect:	I have all my clients' and prospects' mobile phone numbers and whenever I visit Africa. I have barbecues with them on the weekend. So we're doing just fine.
Me:	[Mocking tone] Lucky you, having barbecues on the weekend.
Prospect:	[Silence. Snicker.] Who is this?
Me:	I am impressed, I've never met someone who's lucky enough to barbecue with their prospects in Africa.
Prospect:	You got me there. I sounded like a jerk. I'm sorry.
Me:	Didn't bother me, sounds like you've had a long week.

Prospect: Tell me about it. Listen, I'm on my way out, can you email me and I'll follow up on Monday?

Five minutes later, we arranged a meeting over email.

If I had been in my ego, I could have taken offence at Dave's sarcasm and given up. Instead, I was present. I was able to let his comment pass through me, without judgement, and offer a light-hearted response that came from a centred place.

Egos need conflict like a fire needs oxygen. Your presence acts as a fire extinguisher that snuffs out the drama and judgement that gets in the way of rapport-building.

Innate talent is a myth

Anders Ericsson, a world leading researcher in high performance, makes the case that it's not inherited talent which determines how good we become at something. Instead, it's how hard we're willing to work at it, how much we're willing to deliberately practise something.

Isn't this statement wonderfully empowering? If I can do it, little old me who was scared of her own shadow, then absolutely anyone can sell, including you.

Remember, sales is about your customer, but it starts with you. How you think affects how you feel, what you say, how you act and the results you get. You can learn all the magical advanced sales techniques in the world, but if you're feeling disheartened and desperate, then the highest logic and most sophisticated strategies will not help you. I've been there. It just doesn't work. You're dealing with people and egos; one word spoken from a negative place could turn a warm client into an ice-cold one. It's happened to me! So take control of your mind first and have it serve you.

This process is designed for entrepreneurs, startups and

freelancers who don't have a sales team and have no sales experience. You've learned enough techniques to give you a good foundation to get out there and start growing your sales.

You'll have ups and downs; it's the nature of sales. The difference is now you've got tools to help you dig in, dust yourself off and ignore that paralysing negative conversation so you can keep moving forward. With persistence, you absolutely will win, and keep winning, creating a virtuous cycle.

EPIC ACT: Your seven steps to success

At first, there will be a torrent of activity in your mind when you're with clients because now you're aware of this new process you should be following. When I first started in sales, I would keep a list of the steps in front of me and I would tick each step when I'd completed them.

If ever I was lost or stumbled, I looked at the paper and knew what to do next. Just remember the seven steps, which form the acronym EPIC ACT™. The idea was to make it something inspiring so you'd pursue your passion, do what you love, and live the epic act, that life we all want. My little bit to help you on your journey is teaching you how to sell without being salesy.

Remember the process, EPIC ACT:

> **Ethos**: Sales is about your customer but it starts with you. What is your relationship like with the present moment?
> **Preparation:** If you don't prepare to win, be prepared to fail.
> **Investigation:** Seek first to understand and suspend your self-interest.

Confirm: After understanding their aggravations and ambitions, confirm you understand them.
Add Value: It's your turn to demonstrate how you can add value with your demo or presentation and again in your proposal.
Contribution: Instead of pestering them for feedback, how can you help them?
Take Action: Use a simple close to move forward

Treat every prospect and every person along the buying chain with respect and courtesy. From the receptionist answering the phone to middle managers and CEOs. They all have a need to feel appreciated and understood. It's human nature. Karma will take care of the rest.

Get in touch

Tell me how you get on, I want to know how you're using what you've learned. I love hearing your stories so please email me at anis@mindfulsalestraining.net

If you need more help, then take a look at my online courses, where I teach cold calling, beginner and masterclass sales courses.
http://mindfulsalestraining.net/online-sales-courses/

If you'd like something more bespoke, I offer 1-to-1 coaching on sales and personal growth, so when you have meetings with clients you've got some practise under your belt. Get in touch via anis@mindfulsalestraining.net

Or, if you just want free tips, sign-up to get my weekly email, where I'll send you practical wisdom to get your sales hustle on.
http://mindfulsalestraining.net

Help me empower more people

Finally, if you enjoyed this book and found value in it, please leave an Amazon review for it to help other folks like you grow their sales doing what they love. It would really mean a lot to me if you could help me achieve my mission to help more people.

With love and immense gratitude,

Anis Qizilbash

ACKNOWLEDGEMENTS

Thank you to my wife, Jennifer. She's been the wind beneath my wings, helping me stay afloat in those early days when I decided to forge my own path. This book would be a jumbled mess without her sublime editing skills.

Thank you, readers. You've taken the bold step to do what you love. Your courage and passion inspired me to write this book.

ABOUT THE AUTHOR

Anis Qizilbash is the founder of Mindful Sales Training, which serves mindful inspiration to entrepreneurs and freelancers around the world through a website, email and training programmes. Anis' mission is to help entrepreneurs and freelancers pursuing their passion learn the vital skills they need to grow their sales without being salesy; so they can continue serving the world by doing what they love. She's an inspiring and motivational speaker who empowers people to overcome self-doubt and start doing what they love.

She's happily married to her partner of eight years and mother to a fur baby, Whiskey. She's a voracious reader and enjoys travelling, swimming and running.

RESOURCES

Weekly tips & practical wisdom

Sign-up to receive my weekly emails, where I share tips, techniques and practical wisdom to up your game. You can sign up at www.mindfulsalestraining.net

Lead generation

If you want to learn how to use your phone and email to book more meetings, then check out my Conscious Cold Calling online programme. I teach you where to find leads, what to say and how to stop your monkey mind from sabotaging your success. www.mindfulsalestraining.net/online-sales-courses

EASY Selling

If you want to learn the basic sales skills to get you started, then join me on this online programme. I walk you through

an easy process to steer conversations towards a sale, communicate your value, avoid mistakes that kill sales and present your offer in ways that resonate with your buyers.
www.mindfulsalestraining.net/online-sales-courses

Mindful Sales Masterclass

If you want to up your sales game, Mindful Sales Masterclass teaches the EPIC ACT in depth. If your nerves and limiting beliefs are stopping you from successfully selling, you'll learn different tools to help you get the successful seller mindset. You'll learn advanced questioning techniques, how to prevent objections and much more!
www.mindfulsalestraining.net/online-sales-courses

BIBLIOGRAPHY

[1] Daniel Siegel, *Mindsight: Transform Your Brain with the New Science of Kindness*, (Oneworld Publications, 2011), pp. 26 - 30 of 314 in Kindle edition

[2] David Rock, *Your Brain at Work: Strategies for Overcoming Distraction, Regaining Focus, and Working Smarter All Day Long*, (Harper Collins e-books, 2009), p.6 of 290 in Kindle edition

[3] Daniel Siegel, *Mindsight: Transform Your Brain with the New Science of Kindness*, (Oneworld Publications, 2011), p.258 of 314 in Kindle edition

[4] David Rock, *Your Brain at Work: Strategies for Overcoming Distraction, Regaining Focus, and Working Smarter All Day Long*, (Harper Collins e-books, 2009), pp.77 - 80 of 290 in Kindle edition

[5] Daniel Siegel, *Mindsight: Transform Your Brain with the New Science of Kindness*, (Oneworld Publications, 2011), p.116 of 314 in Kindle edition

[6] Daniel Siegel, *Mindsight: Transform Your Brain with the New Science of Kindness*, (Oneworld Publications, 2011), p.133 of 314 in Kindle edition

[7] Daniel Siegel, *Mindsight: Transform Your Brain with the New Science of Kindness*, (Oneworld Publications, 2011), p.86 of 314 in Kindle edition

[8] Massachusetts General Hospital. "Mindfulness meditation training changes brain structure in eight weeks." ScienceDaily, 21 January 2011

[9] Eckhart Tolle, *The Power of Now: A Guide to Spiritual Enlightenment*, (Yellow Kite, 2001) p.21 of 229 in Kindle edition

[10] Tony Schwartz and Jim Loehr, *The Power of Full Engagement: Managing Energy, Not Time, is the Key to Performance, Health, and Happiness*, (The Free Press, 2003), p.132

[11] [1984] United Kingdom House of Lords 4, [1985] 1 All ER 1025, [1985] AC 905 http://www.bailii.org/uk/cases/UKHL/1984/4.html

[12] Martin Seligman, *Learned Optimism: How to Change Your Mind and Your Life*, (Vintage Books, 1990), p.15 of 292 in Kindle edition

[13] Martin Seligman, *Learned Optimism: How to Change Your Mind and Your Life*, (Vintage Books, 1990), p.217 of 292 in Kindle edition

[14] Mihaly Csikszentmihalyi, *Flow: The Psychology of Happiness*, (Random House,1992), pp.141-142 of 240 in Kindle edition

[15] Brendon Burchard, *Millionaire Messenger: Make a Difference and a Fortune Sharing Your Advice*, (Simon and Schuster, 2011), p.96

[16] Timothy Galloway, *The Inner Game of Tennis: The Ultimate Guide to the Mental Side of Peak Performance*, (Pan Books, 1986), p.111

[17] Andrew Agassi, *Open: An Autobiography*, (Harper Collins, 2009), Location 485 of 7634 in Kindle edition

[18] Mihaly Csikszentmihalyi, *Flow: The Psychology of Happiness*, (Random House, 1992), p.50 of 240 in Kindle edition

[19] IDC Research, *Always Connected: How Smartphones And Social Keep Us Engaged*, (IDC, 2013) http://www.nu.nl/files/IDC-Facebook%20Always%20Connected%20(1).pdf

[20] David Rock, *Your Brain at Work: Strategies for Overcoming Distraction, Regaining Focus, and Working Smarter All Day Long*, (Harper Collins e-books, 2009), p.12 of 290 in Kindle edition

[21] Chet Holmes, *Ultimate Sales Machine: Turbocharge Your Business with Relentless Focus on 12 Key Strategies*, (Portfolio, 2007), p.14 of 245 in Kindle edition

[22] Daniel Levitin, *The Organised Mind: Thinking Straight in the Age of Information Overload*, (Viking, 2014), Location1891 of 9877 in Kindle edition

[23] Tony Schwartz and Jim Loehr, *The Power of Full Engagement: Managing Energy, Not Time, is the Key to Performance, Health, and Happiness*, (The Free Press, 2003), p.60

[24] Tony Schwartz and Jim Loehr, *The Power of Full Engagement: Managing Energy, Not Time, is the Key to Performance, Health, and Happiness*, (The Free Press, 2003), p.67

[25] Harvard Medical School, *Glycemic index and glycemic load for 100+ foods* (Harvard Health Publications, February 2015) http://www.health.harvard.edu/healthy-eating/glycemic_index_and_glycemic_load_for_100_foods

[26] Bob Burg, *Endless Referrals: Network Your everyday Contacts into Sales*, (McGraw Hill, 2006), p.74 of 279 in Kindle edition

[27] Robert Cialdini, *Influence: The Psychology of Persuasion*, (Harper Collins, 1984), p.208

[28] Robert Cialdini, *Influence: The Psychology of Persuasion*, (Harper Collins, 1984), p.209

[29] Tony Buzan, *The Speed Reading Book*, (BBC Active, 2009)

[30] Stephen R. Covey, *The 7 Habits of Highly Effective People*, (Simon & Schuster, 2004), p.237 of 340 in Kindle edition

[31] Abraham Maslow, *A Theory of Human Motivation*, (Psychological Review, 1943), pp. 370 - 396

[32] Brent Adamson et al, *Why self-image matters in B2B sales*, (Harvard Business Review April 2015) https://hbr.org/2015/04/why-self-image-matters-in-b2b-sales?

[33] Robert Cialdini, *Influence: The Psychology of Persuasion*,(Harper Collins, 1984), pp. 58 - 113

[34] Carmine Gallo, *The Presentation Secrets of Steve Jobs: How to Be Insanely Great in Front of Any Audience*, (McGraw Hill, 2010), pp.39-47

[35] Neil Rackman, *SPIN Selling*, (Gower Publishing Ltd, 1995), p.34

Printed in Great Britain
by Amazon